FIVE KISSES FOR A PENNY

ABOUT THE AUTHOR

Dee May was born to spiritualist parents without, in her younger days, being greatly affected by their beliefs. But in the course of her adult life spent visiting, living, and working in more that twenty countries, from Canada in the west to Pakistan in the east, she encountered evidence of a spirit world too powerful to be ignored.

Her first book, *A Necklace of Orange Seeds,* concerning one of her incarnations, was written as a novel based on traumatic experiences with native witch-doctors in the rain forest of central Africa. These episodes caused her to search for explanations and become deeply involved in the study and practice of spiritualism.

Five Kisses for a Penny is the true story of a different episode in Dee's life, strangely related to Africa, telling the where and when, just as it happened, and accurate in every detail.

Also by Dee May

A Necklace of Orange Seeds
Dandelion Clocks
Not All Prisoners are in Cages
Crossing The Barrier
The Pit of the Wild Seas

FIVE KISSES FOR A PENNY

DEE MAY

CANDLELIGHT PRESS

Published by CANDLELIGHT PRESS 1994
11 Wrotham Road, Broadstairs,
Kent CT10 1QG

Copyright © Dee May 1994

French Translation Copyright ©
Julia Lopez 1994
All rights reserved

No part of this book may be reproduced
in whole or in part
(except in the case of reviews),
without written permission from the
publisher.

British Library Cataloguing in
Publication Data

May, Dee
Five Kisses for a Penny.
I. Title
133.91092

ISBN 1-873563-30-2

Cover design by Phillip May
Printed by Whitstable Litho Printers Ltd.
Millstrood Road, Whitstable Kent CT5 3PP
(01227) 262311

For
two very special men
with love

ACKNOWLEDGEMENTS

My grateful thanks are extended to Mrs Doreen Law, her son Steve and daughter Vicky, for their ready acceptance of me, and their help in making it possible for Jimmy and I to reach inner stillness.

My thanks also to Margaret Collier whose friendship and knowledge of spiritual matters, supported me all the way through.

And deepest thanks to my husband, Phillip, who gave me his love, and cried with me when the long haul was over.

INTRODUCTION

This is the true story of crisis apparitions experienced by Dee May who, after forty-seven years, was able to trace and comfort a dying man. He needed her understanding and peace, and this is what she was able to give.

Jimmy wanted Dee the first moment he saw her and called her Echo, but she belonged to Phil who had known her since childhood. Neither man knew they had fought for this woman through many incarnations; and the triangle would be endlessly repeated, unless they remembered the plans they had made in the *bardo*.

We see the story through the eyes of Dee, who was forced to choose between the two men. We see also, the gradual awareness of other life-times, the awakening of knowledge and the evolvement of these three people to where the men could respect each other and work through their karma, leaving all of them free for the next stage of their journey.

Virginia Eastland

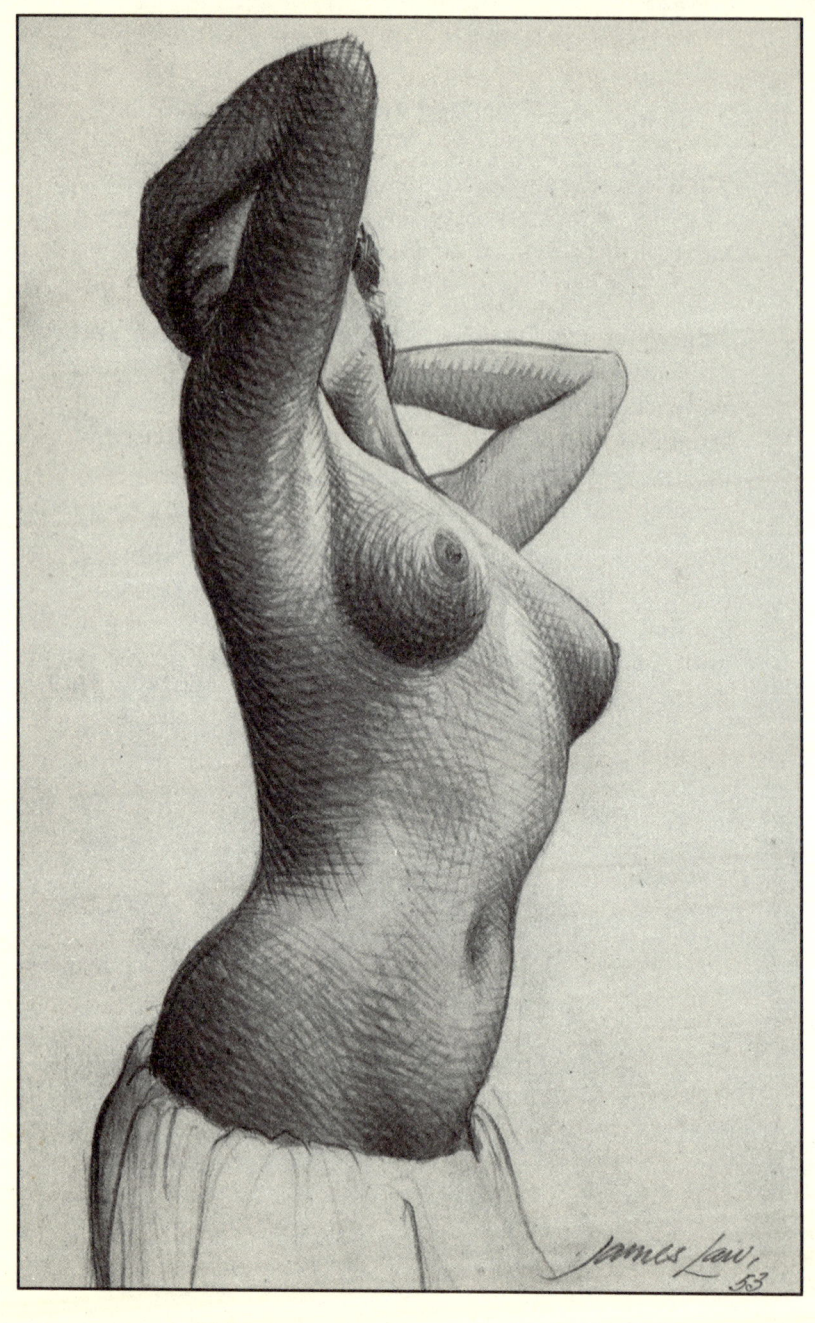

'DOROTHEA' *Sepia Wash Drawing by James Law*

One

On the afternoon of Tuesday, 1st December 1992, I climbed the stairs to my "African Hut" closely followed by medium Margaret Collier. For a couple of months we had been hoping to contact my parents whose passing had occurred a number of years earlier, but what neither she nor I knew on this Tuesday afternoon was that an incredible story was about to unfold: the revelation of karma between two men and a woman, which had nothing to do with my parents.

Back in 1978, and which I now know to be part of the karma, I had transformed the top floor of my house to resemble the inside of an African hut. It was a gesture of defiance after surviving a traumatic experience in the Ituri rain forest of northern Zaire which, several years later I wrote about, calling the book *A Necklace of Orange Seeds*. But on this afternoon in 1992 a very different part of the story was to emerge proving that just as fear may feed on itself, love can break down the toughest barrier with little or no awareness of force.

We settled ourselves on the settee, comfortable in the warm room and with each other. After a while various family members made themselves known, which was encouraging. Although still early it was growing dark outside with rain beginning to spatter the windows when Margaret's voice changed from matter-of-fact to incredulous. "There's somebody else here," she said. "He's not one of the family and he's a bit hesitant to come through. Dee... it's somebody you were connected to, before you were married to Phil."

Time seemed to stand still. Someone else was talking to me, telling a story, and I was listening. Margaret's voice went on but the other voice was clearer, wrapping itself round my brain, hypnotising me so that I could absorb what was being said and understand the necessity for my return to the earthplane this time. It was going like this:

"Remember Dee. There *was* someone else. Someone you thought had died a long time ago. A man you were desperately in love with down a long tunnel of time that gradually filled up and covered him over. Yet lately there have been dreams, disturbing dreams. You cannot deny that."

The voice was right. I could not deny that, but remembering would be painful and I wasn't sure if I was ready to cope with it. I switched my mind to thinking of Phil. I first met Phil in the summer of 1939 when I was only a kid with a head full of dreams and knights in shining armour, and he was a man already grown, and had been round the world in the Royal Navy – yet there was magic between us. A long time and many miles later, when he'd got to know me, and was sure it would be received it the way it was meant, he said: "You were a skinny little girl, with nothing but a beautiful smile going for you, yet you got to somewhere inside me that nobody else had been able to reach. And it frightened the hell out of me."

I tried to listen to Margaret. "There's a lot of emotion here," she was saying. "This man is afraid of being rejected, you've rejected him before, but he says it was not your fault. It was his; and circumstances. He wants you to know that he loves you very much and is always with you."

She must be talking about Jimmy I thought. Yes, I had rejected him, partly because of convention although I had been prepared to fly in the face of it, but mainly because I met Phil again and was forced to make a choice and there had been no way of explaining that I couldn't bear to be parted from either of them. I loved them both and knew that deep down inside I would always mourn the loss of whichever one I rejected.

The voice took over:

"You are absolutely right. The man is certainly Jimmy. James Victor Law, and you met towards the end of the war. April 11th, 1944 to be exact, when you were nineteen years old."

The voice was right. I remembered burning the date into my mind at the time but had not thought of it for many years, and now it seemed that I was being split in two, one half talking to the other, my subconscious or higher self – I was unable to tell which. But one thing was certain: Jimmy was back in my life and not about to be ignored.

I had always known that something wonderful would happen when I was nineteen although I didn't know it was about to happen, that specific evening in April, as I walked towards the Odeon dance-hall in Canterbury. It had been a lousy day. My head ached and I was fed up. The teleprinter machines at the G.P.O. where I worked had clattered since early morning and the pile of telegrams to send had been endless. It was not this that was bugging me, I loved the work; it was the long dragging business of the war and the fact that the airman I thought I was in love with had been away in South Africa for more than three years. And Phil, my knight in shining armour, had disappeared off the face of the earth.

The dance-hall was crowded, packed with servicemen of all nationalities but none of them suited my mood, it would be better to go home than waste my time here...

Then Jimmy walked in.

It was as though he was surrounded by shock waves so that I felt him, those few seconds before seeing him, and magnetism shot between us.

He was in army uniform. He took off his cap and

Five Kisses for a Penny

walked into the cloakroom. Quite suddenly the whole world looked different and I accepted the next man who asked me to dance. It was the act of a drowning girl, knowing oblivion was coming, an oblivion I recognized but did not understand. I looked up at the balcony (the dance-hall had once been an old theatre) and this soldier, this magnetic man was watching my every movement, sending out the unspoken message: 'You're mine. Did you think I would let you forget?'

I left the dance floor and he must have left the balcony at the same time for we met at the foot of the stairs. It was the beginning of a compulsion that would last for the rest of our lives.

It was a shock to discover Jimmy was married. I had taken off my engagement ring, which was noticed by one of my friends. "I suppose you know that soldier you're going around with is married," she said.

I waved my hand airily. "Of course I know. But I don't care." I didn't know, and I did care. I cared very much indeed – and it hurt.

"Why didn't you tell me you were married?" I accused him later.

"I was afraid of losing you," he said simply. "I love you Echo, and I'll make everything right. You'll see."

I believed what he said, not just because I wanted to believe it, but because I knew he believed it himself. In any case there was no turning back. There was nowhere to go after Jimmy, the man who was calling me Echo, the echo of love down the passage of time.

"Dee, are you all right?"

Margaret's voice sounded hollow, a million miles away. I brought myself back from the past. "Yes. I was just thinking. I know the man who came through. I had a nightmare about him a long time ago which I've never forgotten. To say it was a nightmare is an understatement. It was terrifyingly real and I felt sure he was dead.

"He was on a railway platform and behind him was a train in the station. It was dark and he was dressed in old-fashioned clothes, a cut away jacket and a tall top-hat. He didn't say anything. He just looked at me and held out his hand. He was drawing me to him and I knew if I took his hand that I wouldn't wake up in the morning. I would have crossed from the land of the living to the world of the dead.

"It was freezing cold and I was screaming for Phil. I screamed so much I woke myself up yet only a croak was coming out of my throat. I closed my eyes and was immediately back at the railway station – and he was there – looking at me and holding out his hand. I wanted so much to go to him yet I was terrified of not waking up. Again I began screaming, and screaming, awoke. Phil still slept beside me and all the time I could feel myself being drawn back to Jimmy.

"This happened three times and in the end I got out of bed and sat awake in a chair for the rest of the night."

There was not a lot to say after this. My mind

Five Kisses for a Penny 7

was seething with thoughts of Jimmy and wondering why he'd been walking into my dreams lately, or had I been walking in his? Was he dead or was he alive somewhere? It was impossible to tell.

Words are flat and times have changed so much it's difficult to portray how it feels to be young and living one day at a time through a war. Emotions are heightened by danger and every second is precious. People come into your life who in the normal way you would never have met. They smile, and get right inside you. You smile back, and metaphorically their arms enfold you. There is no time for questions, they are unimportant. What use are questions if tomorrow you may not be here to deal with the answers? You take everyone at face value. What you see is what you get and what you get is the very best a person can give because he feels as you do – time could be running out – tomorrow may never come.

The summer of 1944 was a magical time. Jimmy and I were in love, not only with each other but with life – and love and life know no boundaries. They're like a song that's there at the back of your mind, constantly forcing itself to the surface – making you smile – and others smile with you.

That summer is now a blur in my mind, a blur of walks in the rain, bicycle rides in the sun, wild flowers growing, slim brown hands, warm lips meeting, senses melting and the agony of parting. There was always something to take him away, some training course or other, something new he needed to learn for fighting a war. But there were compensations: love letters to write and receive, and telegrams. Telegrams were the backbone of communication. They could be sent for one shilling and be delivered inside of one hour. And for one more penny you could buy five kisses. Mine always came with five kisses. Five kisses for a penny. We put them on all of our love letters too.

Then came the day we'd been dreading. He was posted abroad. His address changed to B.A.O.R. British Army of the Rhine. There were occasional letters but mostly little brown cards with official printing on them and a dotted line where the soldier could place his signature. There was no way of knowing *where* Jimmy was but at least I knew he was alive.

Some time in early 1945 he arrived at our house in Thanington. I say 'arrived', although I was unable to see him. My parents were spiritualists and Mother startled us all one evening by saying that Jimmy was with us. He was wearing a long khaki overcoat. "He's been injured," she said. "It's his head and the side of his face. But he's going to be all right."

A few weeks later he was home on leave and I was happy again. It was dark in the evenings, and cold. Searchlights were sweeping the sky as we walked home from dances. He carried my sandals in his greatcoat pocket and held my hands to keep them warm. It was not the reawakening love we had known in the summer, but the deep down awareness that we belonged together, had always belonged together, and nothing could ever change that.

We determined then, that when the war was over, we would never allow anything to part us again. And while he was with me I could believe what we said, yet each time he left, and I was alone, the frightening blackness of fear held me rigid: he was married – the world of convention was too big to fight – how could we ever not lose each other?

Desolation crept in.

But each time he came back his warmth smoothed all the rough edges. He held me close to his body, hands in my hair, lips on my cheeks, eye-lids and finally seeking my mouth, dwelling there until I felt there was no tomorrow, and if there was, I would be with him because it had always been this way and nothing was going to change it.

All through that year on his subsequent leaves we were together. There were hot summer days when he sketched me in orchards, down by the river, awake or asleep. Any time and in any place. He was an artist and would be working again when the misery of wartime was over. And as for his being married, what did it matter? He would not be able to divorce his wife, she had done nothing to deserve it. But we could live together. He would rent a studio in Wincheap Street. He had earmarked a place already. We would change our names and pretend we were married. He would send me a list to choose from.

And he did.

He was back now in France and more letters came, each with five kisses. He was painting a portrait in oils, he said, a portrait of me from a photograph. One letter ran to twenty-six pages, some of it explaining that part of his next leave must be spent with his wife, to settle things up, but not to worry, we would have a couple of days together – and he sent me the date.

On the appointed day I rushed to the station to meet him. It was my week for late duties but I managed to get there in time. The place was dark and deserted and not a single soul stepped down from the train. I was so sick at heart that I pushed my bicycle all the way home, unable to ride it for the tears that prevented me from seeing the road clearly. I just wanted to die. He didn't love me. I would never see him again.

But he hadn't deserted me for there on the mantle-piece was a telegram saying: SORRY UNABLE TO MAKE IT. PROMISE TO SPEND ALL OF NEXT LEAVE WITH YOU. MY LOVE IS FOR EVER. XXXXX

Tears started anew. Why wasn't I given this message at work? I had been there all day. If there were telegrams for any of us we were always given them. It would have been disappointing enough without all the build-up. Oh just let me die...

But I got over it, and letters came, and poems, and best of all the news I'd been waiting for. His time with the Army was almost finished. He would be home by Christmas – for good.

Five Kisses for a Penny

I was over the moon.

He came home by Christmas, bringing my portrait. But he was not here to stay. The Army was demanding another three months. We were to have nine short days together then he must go back to France until March.

Is it possible to drown without actually drowning? For that's how it felt. Confusion robbed me of words, yet heightened perception. We tried to talk but talk brought thoughts too appalling to linger over. Another three months. It might as well have been three decades – three lifetimes – three million years.

I remember thinking: What we need is a Rainmaker, someone to make miracles happen. But we were in Never-Never land where nothing begins and nothing ends, a limbo land of lost lovers. Jimmy looked like a little boy who had been beaten by bullies, and was unable to do anything about it but hate them. How I looked I don't know, but I felt completely scooped out inside and around me was a permanent hole cut out of the world. Each time he kissed me the hole grew bigger. I could not stop crying. His tears were unshed but the heart-stopping hollows under his eyes, and his hot swollen lips said it all. It was easy to understand why there were suicide pacts.

We went to the New Year's Eve dance at the Odeon and although I'm searching my memory I can remember nothing about it. He was to leave for France on January the 4th. That's all I can think of. It must have filled my mind to the exclusion of everything else.

It's a good thing none of us can see into the future for it would colour our perception of the present, and the present is all we can bank on and should never be wasted. We all know the old saying 'You're a long time dead', which tells us we should make the most of each day while we have it; what I didn't know then and *do* know now is that we are here for a purpose, and that we return as many times as is necessary for us to recognize this. Most things can be learned on other planes but until we have worked out relationships here, we are unable to progress further.

In the *bardo*, where we spend *life between lives*, we see the mistakes we have made and plan how to rectify them. We may not be strong enough to stick to our plans, but at least we can try.

Our biggest problem is that we return with limited knowledge. We are working blind as it were, except for occasional glimpses, and what I am trying to show here is just one example of the many lifetimes it can take before we get some of it right.

On the night of Thursday, January 3rd 1946, I had no idea it would be forty-seven years before I saw Jimmy again and that it would take all that time for me to understand why.

Two

On the morning of Friday, 4th January 1946, I was in the telegraph-room at work. We had clung together the night before unable to say the word 'good-bye', and the hours were dragging like long heavy freight trains. Then the telephone rang.

"I just wanted to hear your voice," Jimmy said. "I'm on my way but it's so hard to go."

"I know. I know," was all I could say for the boulder in my throat.

"I love you Echo, I love you."

I could hear his voice breaking and there was nothing I could do. The line crackled and went dead.

Down in the rest-room I hung out of the second floor window looking into Stour Street feeling sure he would pass this way to the bus station at the bottom of the town. After fifteen minutes there was no sign of him and I should have gone back to the telegraph-room but there was no way I could do it. Instead, I put on my coat and went into the street.

The weather was cold and the air was made of thick fog – so thick that it was impossible to see from one side of the street to the other. I walked down one side trying to see across, then back up the other the same way. He had not been at the bus station and was nowhere in sight. I was devastated. There was nothing to do but return to the office.

For the rest of that day my thoughts clanked against one another and even in sleep they gave me no peace – they caused a traumatic dream: I was in my home, reading a telegram from Jimmy. The words were big and clear; and they read:

GO TO THE BUS STOP TODAY AND LIE DOWN IN THE ROAD SO THAT PEOPLE WILL THINK YOU ARE DEAD. I WILL COME PAST IN MY ARMY LORRY AND PICK UP YOUR BODY AND TAKE IT WITH ME. WE WILL FIND SOMEWHERE TO LIVE WHERE NOBODY KNOWS US. IF YOU DO THIS FOR ME I SHALL KNOW THAT YOU LOVE ME. IF YOU ARE NOT THERE WHEN I PASS IN THE LORRY I SHALL KNOW THAT YOU DONT AND WE WILL NEVER SEE EACH OTHER AGAIN. XXXXX

Frantically I ran to the bus stop and laid down in the road. It all seemed perfectly logical. People walked by and took no notice. I lay there for a long long time and nothing happened. Then I checked on the telegram to make sure I was doing exactly as he had said, and discovered to my horror that according to the date I should have been there the previous day. The telegram had arrived too late. He had already passed by in his

Five Kisses for a Penny 15

army lorry and had gone away thinking I didn't love him. And there was no way of knowing where he had gone.

It was the prelude to years of traumatic dreams of searching for Jimmy in a fog-filled world, where he believed that I did not love him and I could not prove that I did.

On the evening of Saturday, 19th January 1946, Phil walked back into my life. Phillip Robert Stephen May. I was at the Odeon and it was the first time I had been anywhere but work since the day Jimmy left.

From being the child Phil remembered I had grown into a woman. Seven years is a long time and a lot of ground had been covered but the magic was still there. In the years before Jimmy I had thought of Phil often: not seriously, for he was out of my reach, but in a day-dreaming fashion. He would always be there when I needed to be rescued – the knight with the shining armour. And here he was now... asking me to dance... I could hardly believe it.

With the benefit of hind-sight, it is easy to see what has brought each one of us to our present situation, but when we start out in life we are without this benefit, and must therefore chart our way through the minefield of living where we can make all the mistakes we previously made if nobody steps in to divert us. Yet also I feel that somewhere inside us there must be a residue of past events, some little trigger that puts up the warning notice 'TREAD CAREFULLY', which eventually we recognize and accept.

This time round it happened to me but none of it came easy.

Somewhere near the end of that evening of dancing with Phil he told me he must leave. He had a date with a barmaid called Lynne.

"I'll save the last dance for you if you come back," I said.

To this day I don't know how those words came out of my mouth. I was much too shy to have said them, and much too much in love with Jimmy.

But Phil came back. And we had the last dance. And he walked me home, which was about two miles in the opposite direction from where he was living.

It was the beginning of my change of direction although I was totally unaware of it at the time.

The next week was exciting. The three following were traumatic – to say the least. Phil wanted me to marry him. And what Phil wants he sets out to get and if he's heard of the word 'No' he has no conception of its meaning.

I told him about Jimmy. Not once, but many times. I told him everything, all that we meant to each other.

"I've loved you longer, and I love you more than he ever could," was always his answer.

He gave me until the middle of February to make up my mind. Jimmy was due home in March. I didn't know what to do. How could I choose one man knowing by now that I didn't want to be parted from either? And strangely, although

Five Kisses for a Penny 17

their temperaments were different they looked so much alike, both 6ft tall, with very dark hair and green eyes.

There had not been time to get to know Phil on our first brief encounter and now I was being torn between him and Jimmy, as though I'd been involved emotionally with both men before. Until meeting Phil again I was not aware of the strength of the attraction. He was equally magnetic – if not more so than Jimmy. I was being tortured and every day became worse.

I kept charting the reasons for and against being with each man and eventually Jimmy came out on the down side: He was married already. Perhaps he would not leave his wife. And if he did, could 'living in sin' possibly work out in the conventional society to which we belonged? And most important of all: did he really love me in the way I loved him?

My answer to the last question was 'No. He did not.' The love I had for him could not possibly be equalled. On this I based my decision. I would marry Phil because his love for me was greater than my love for him and therefore he would never be able to hurt me.

Looking back it was a strange way to be thinking then but in the light of what I have since learned, it was not so strange: Jimmy has hurt me in numerous lifetimes and this present one was designed for repaying his karmic debt. But the final choice had to be mine. Only I could help him to do it. The inner knowledge must have been there, yet only through Phil, whose knowledge must have been greater, could the plans the three of us made in the *bardo* be put into effect.

On the afternoon of Saturday, 29th June 1946, Phil and I were married at Thanington and a new way of life was about to begin.

Living with Phil was not easy. His possessiveness knew no boundary but then, neither did his love. I thought of him as the elder brother I had always wanted and the father I had needed and never had.

My father was the quietest, kindest, most perfect man I have ever known. I loved him passionately but he was remote. He worked so hard for us when I was a child that he had nothing of himself left to give.

Perhaps that is not quite how it was but it's the way that I saw it. I longed to be held in his arms and fussed over. It didn't matter that I had all of this from my mother – I needed it from him. But I had long passed this stage when Phil and I married so it was like being given all my birthday and Christmas presents in one.

It was a shock to discover after a number of years, that although my conscious mind was welded firmly to Phil, my subconscious was never going to accept the fact, and every so often would hammer me with one of my 'searching dreams', as I came to think of them. Dreams in which I was searching for Jimmy.

There was no pattern of circumstances to

Five Kisses for a Penny 19

account for the intrusions – and intrusions is what they were. They intruded upon my life. They never let me forget. They put me right back into the situation I had been in the night of the first bad dream, the day after searching for Jimmy in the fog. The dreams were never the same, but in all of them I would be searching. I might see his Army lorry and run after it, only to see it disappear round a corner. I could be asking people questions and be told where he was, only to find he had gone somewhere else. I might catch sight of him, fight my way through to him, only to discover the person was somebody else and *not* him. In all the searchings I was able to reach him just once and when he saw me he turned away without speaking. The trauma never diminished. If anything, it became worse. He had taken possession of me in all my dimensions. That was the frightening part.

It was impossible to understand what was happening at the time, but the reason became clear a few months ago when we met again and were able to talk. He told me that when he arrived back in England in March 1946 he felt he had nothing to live for. The Manchester streets were full of fog. He couldn't face going back to his wife. He had lost Echo, the girl that he loved. She was going to marry a man called Phil. He could do nothing to prevent this from happening, but he didn't have to accept it. He would never let go of her.

He reminded me of the language 'Interglossa'

(an international language based on well-known Greek and Latin roots, devised by Lancelot Hogben), that he had been teaching me, and of the word 'Philo' denoting lover and loving which we used all the time. Armed with the knowledge that this was something only he and I shared, he was able to cradle my mind and hold me close enough to go on with his life.

I told him of the 'searching dreams' that had caused me so much anguish over so many years and which petered out some time around 1951. He said they must have been caused by his utter desolation and anger, coupled with the frustration of being powerless to change the course of events. He said he was sorry for causing me pain. It had not been intended. He also said that in 1951 his life changed direction. He became involved with another woman and married again.

We had so little time together that I forgot to tell him of the nightmare in which he held out his hand at the railway station, trying to claim me from Phil. I've traced back the year to 1953. And I have positive proof that his mind was with me at that time. But this is something I will talk about later.

After a number of years and four children Phil suggested we try to find Jimmy. "I would like to meet the man you once loved," he said. "I've often wondered about my rival. He must have been special to have claimed your attention."

But I didn't want to visit the past. Any wounds

Five Kisses for a Penny

that I had, had healed long ago and I wasn't prepared to have them reopened. My memories of Jimmy tasted like summer, and although perhaps only memories of memories, I wanted to keep it that way. It is never wise to go back for you are not the same person, and the place where you stood is inhabited by strangers. This was something I could not explain to the man I had married. Jimmy was there warm inside me but he never took away anything I felt for the children or their father. He was just there.

To write this book is not easy. Perhaps no book is easy but I've been told that Jimmy will help me with this one. And this is indeed happening. Several phrases, which I would not normally use, have been put into my mind already, yet sometimes there is a complete blank and yesterday afternoon was one of these times. It is very seldom that I have several hours in which to write and extremely annoying when the shutters go up and nothing can squeeze its way through. I needed something to follow on from the last paragraph I had written and nothing appropriate presented itself and finally I gave up in frustration. Then early this morning something really amazing happened:

In a dream I was driving along in my car and Phil was driving behind me in his. I was wearing a jacket which had to be delivered to someone. Phil said he would park his car and wait.

I found the woman I was looking for. She was wearing a white apron and working at the end of a long corridor in a hospital. I called out to her and she shouted something back which I was unable to hear although I knew it to be in the negative. I took off the jacket and held it out but she wouldn't accept it. Someone gave me a pair of blue ear-rings which I put in my ears. Then someone else came and took them away. There was a lot more to the dream but my main concern was for Phil. I wanted to get back to him but could not find his car.

The hospital stood on its own yet was surrounded by long narrow streets of terraced houses, and there was nowhere a car could be parked. All the streets led to the hospital and I was frantically searching from one to the other fully aware that as I went down one of them I could be missing Phil who may be coming up another. In effect, I was searching for Phil in the same state of panic as in so many dreams for so many years I had searched for Jimmy, although this thought was not in my mind.

Then quite suddenly I was awake and Jimmy was with me, holding me tight. It was the most incredible thing I have ever experienced. I could feel his body pressed close to mine, the body of a person from the world of spirit. It is impossible to find any words to describe this sensation.

A few moments later he moved and stood looking at me. Then he was gone. It was the strangest feeling for although I did not hear his voice I knew he was explaining that he was aware of my panic and was keeping me safe. He was saying that sleep made no difference. He was there all the time and knew what was going on in my mind. It was only then I remembered what I'd been dreaming and realized that he knew I was searching for Phil in the same way as so many times I had once searched for him.

It gave me a great deal of food for thought.

Everything we dream has a meaning but sometimes unravelling the dreams is like trying to solve Chinese puzzles. I already knew the jacket and the blue ear-rings were especially significant. Jackets are symbolic of our earthly bodies (a covering for the spiritual body) and the colour blue, although a spiritual colour, can be cancelled out by the material, (ear-rings for instance). Yet when talking to Margaret later I learned that what had seemed a pretty straightforward sort of dream, needing little unravelling, was in fact much more complex than I thought. It contained a great deal of hidden information of which I should take notice.

We never give up our freedom of choice but it's quite frightening to think of the decisions one makes in dreams, and the decisions we allow to be made for us by those on the spirit side.

In the dream (I had left my body as we all do at night, and gone to the spirit side), I took off the jacket and was trying to get it accepted. The woman was calling out something which I knew to be negative. The blue ear-rings I had put in were preventing me from hearing, but only because I did not want to hear. I wanted the jacket accepted because I wanted to stay on the spirit side, although I was not aware of this. I was not aware of being on the spirit side. Had the woman taken the jacket I would not have returned to the earthplane. So basically, by refusing, she was protecting me.

Apparently I was confused in the dream – having an argument with myself and although I was not conscious of it, Jimmy was telling me of his sadness over the whole issue with me; of the space in his life; and I needed to be there for him to do it. The panic I felt was because of listening to him yet at the same time wanting Phil with me if I were to stay. I didn't want to return but Jimmy brought me back to Phil with his love. It was not my time to stay. There is still a lot of work for me to do here and a lot about him that he wants me to write.

As Margaret and I continued to talk Jimmy told us that in the short time he has been over he has learnt ten times more about himself than he knew before and that I am spending a lot of my time there with him, and will see the side of him I have never known, but will get to know and love. It's important to him that I understand this. He wants me to move around parts of his life and all he did with me in mind. He says I have not reached this point yet. What he wants me to do, when he has made me aware of it, is to emphasise his life as a man, with me always there in the background. Although not able to be with me, he has held me – holding me close to his heart. He compared every woman he met, with me, and he is sad to say this had a lot to do with his unhappiness for they were never able to measure up. He insists that I

Five Kisses for a Penny

put this in and also he wants it known that these comparisons were the cause of a self-inflicted bad passage through life. No one else was to blame. And he realizes also, that had he and I married it would not have lasted for I was on a higher plane and he was self-centred, his attitude one of self righteousness, which is something he is now trying to work through. Everything that happened between the three of us, he, Phil and I, had to happen the way it did, for him to make progress. This book, he says, is much more than a love story, it is a spiritual story which will enlighten a great many people.

As I write this I am constantly having to change my words. It's as though they are being sorted out and dictated to me. But there is not only one voice, there are two. The other belongs to Grey Owl who, as I stood hesitating on the brink, made himself known and pushed me into starting this book. These are his words:

"I am the clouds in the sky – the eternal living clouds. I stand in the doorway and you do not listen. You step aside. The path is too hard. Nothing is achieved successfully without work. Come closer to me. You shall succeed. Be not afraid. Life will go on. Your loved ones liveth on the other side of the curtain. What is there to be afraid of? The air is cool and fresh – the mountains green. We will help once you begin to help yourself – your mother and father also. They look upon you now. Begin the task today. It will be worth while."

Three

One night, shortly after first meeting Jimmy, I dreamed we were living together. I could see the place clearly: an almost bare room up a long narrow passageway off a street in Montmartre. Jimmy was an artist (as he was in this present life before joining the Army) and I was his model and lover. We were cold and poor and had nothing to eat and Jimmy was out trying to sell one of his paintings. I was waiting for him to come back. One end of the room was curtained off and behind this was a low trestle bed where we slept.

Although only short, I remembered the dream for it was particularly vivid and the name of the place unknown to me at the time. It was only later that I discovered Montmartre was, and still is, an artists' quarter of Paris.

In the years that followed I often wondered about the significance of the dream and learned only recently, in past life regression, that it wasn't a dream at all: Jimmy and I have spent many lives together, and this was but one of

Five Kisses for a Penny 27

them. I also learned that Phil has been involved in these lifetimes and that he and Jimmy have 'crossed swords' many times.

The first instance of having lived before was made known to me shortly after returning from Scotland where Phil and I spent our honeymoon. We stayed in a little place called North Berwick, simply because we had no choice: Phil had to rejoin his ship, H.M.S. Bullfinch, at that time clearing underwater obstructions in harbours around this area – obstructions left over from the war.

We had married on the Saturday and travelled to Scotland on Sunday for Phil's return to the Bullfinch on Monday evening. As it happened, the ship stayed around this area for three weeks and although Phil was away every day and able to come ashore for only a couple of hours each evening, we felt an uncanny affinity with Scotland which almost matched our affinity with each other.

The ship's next port of call was Preston. It was only when we met again there that we knew how desperately homesick we were for Scotland. And only when I went back home to wait for a telegram telling me where next to meet Phil, that I learned the reason why: we had lived in Scotland before – in another lifetime.

My mother was reflective when she told me of this. "You and Phil were lovers in that lifetime," she said. "You were married to a different man, and he murdered you both."

Naturally I wanted to know the details: Who

was the man? What did he do?

All she would say was: "He ran a lance through both of you. You will learn of the man and the reason for his action when the time is right."

She was a wise woman. I know now that life has to run its course. We can learn only when we are ready to accept, and I could not have accepted then what she could have told me. It has come little by little in its own time, and with it an understanding of how close is the relationship of passionate love to hate.

In August of this year, 1993, because of an escalation of unusual events I decided to have a past life regression. Until then I had never been particularly interested in the past, the present being the only thing one can bank on seeming much more important. The future would be interesting, yes, but is it wise to know what is in store for us? I think not. Were it not what we wanted it would certainly have an adverse effect on the present. However, the past is a different proposition, it can no longer hurt us and *could* yield valuable information: this was my reasoning.

To say I was apprehensive when embarking on this venture is probably the correct adjective but Keith Surtees quietly and smoothly put me at ease, his voice allaying my fears and giving me confidence. As I lay on his couch he took me gradually into the past, at all times giving me freedom of choice. There was a stairway to climb at the top of which was a corridor of closed doors.

Five Kisses for a Penny

Did I feel like entering any of them?

There was a door on the right which demanded attention yet on entering the room there was nothing – nothing that is, that I wanted to pursue. The room had been cleared of all remembrance. Even the window, curved at the top, was bare, and emphasising this bareness were the scrubbed white boards of the floor. And yet... there was something... something hiding at the back of my mind – a memory of passion but above all – great sadness. (I was to learn of this at a later date.)

On closing the door of this room I crossed the corridor and entered another, finding myself in Montmartre, seeing the room there I had known so well, and experiencing the apprehension of waiting for Jimmy's return – would he have food or would he be carrying the picture he went out to sell?

I did not want to know.

Back in the corridor with its rows of closed doors, none of which looked particularly inviting, there appeared a door with a light around it which had not been there before, or perhaps I had not noticed. It was right at the very end and as I walked towards it, it opened of its own accord, showing grass covered ground and high grey stone towers. The place looked strangely familiar as I walked through the doorway and gazed wonderingly up at the walls of a castle. Then came a pang of something I recognized quickly as fear. This castle was my home. It was situated on the border between England and

Scotland and what had gone on there was horrifyingly chilling.

For a moment I wanted to turn away but the necessity to learn more rooted me to the spot. I was *outside* the castle, which was strictly forbidden. I should have been *inside*. I was being torn between two people – two men. I could feel the love I had for them both, the desperation. But I'd broken the rules and the time for punishment was fast approaching.

The scene changed in as much as I was studying a man on a horse. He was a tall, good-looking young man, and he sat very straight on his horse, a long lance held easily in his left hand, his very easiness causing me tension.

I wished he would move but he was utterly still, which filled me with horror, for I knew without any doubt whatsoever that he was the man who had killed Phil and me.

I heard Keith asking if I would like to move on, saying that what I was seeing was in the past and there was no need to stay. But I was transfixed, my heart thumping wildly. Having come this far I wanted to view the actual scene – there was no turning back.

For some reason I was spared the grisly details. What I saw next was two writhing figures, a man and a girl, facing each other on the ground, trying to touch hands. The girl was me. I was still alive but unable to get up. The man was Phil, and in the same situation, except that I could feel his agony in trying to reach me. The man on the horse sat coldly watching the plight of those on the ground.

It is only during the past few months, and this very gradually, that the identity of the man on the horse has become a conviction. I know who he is, although I should say 'was', and it makes no difference to my love for him for I understand his passionate hate was akin to love.

At the time of Jimmy's first contact with me in December 1992, as Margaret and I sat in my African Hut, I was attending the Belmont Centre in Ramsgate each week for meditation and spiritual development. The group I was in had reached the stage of taking guided journeys to the world of spirit and one evening, shortly after Jimmy's communication, Morton Healey said: "We will go to the meadow and through the archway again, so think of someone on the other side that you would like to see – build them up – try to picture them in every detail."

I could feel my father and smell the smoke of his cigarette and wondered if there was something in particular he wanted to say, so I said, "*Hello, Dad, is there something you want to tell me?*"

He didn't answer.

I thought he must know that Jimmy had contacted me so I said, "*I would very much like to see you, Dad, and I don't want to hurt your feelings, but I'd like to follow-up on what Margaret was telling me on Tuesday.*"

He still didn't answer, but the cigarette smoke became stronger.

"You are in the meadow and we are building an archway," Morton said. "The person you are going to see is beyond the archway and will be walking towards you."

I tried to picture Jimmy but it was forty-six years since I'd seen him and I couldn't remember a single individual feature on which to build his face.

"Go through the archway," Morton said.

There was no one walking towards me. Jimmy was right there. He was waiting inside the archway.

He smiled, and immediately it was as though I had seen him only yesterday.

I wondered how I could have forgotten how he smiled. Everything about him was so familiar. He put his arms around me... neither of us spoke.

"Ask the person you have met to remind you of something in connection with them that you have forgotten," Morton said. "It will be proof to you that you are really with them."

I waited, not knowing what to say. It all sounded so unrealistic.

Then Jimmy showed me a book. It was a poetry book with an embossed dark-green cover. He reminded me of the poems he used to write for me and of one in particular that I loved.

I tried to remember the title: it was either *Three Dreams* or *Three Shadows*.

"*It was 'Three Shadows'*," he said.

Then I remembered every word:

THREE SHADOWS

I looked and saw your eyes in the shadow of
 your hair,
As a traveller sees the stream in the shadow
 of the wood:–
And I said, "My faint heart sighs, ah me! to
 linger there,
To drink deep and to dream in that sweet
 solitude."

I looked and saw your heart in the shadow
 of your eyes,
As a seeker sees the gold in the shadow of
 the stream;
And I said, "Ah, me! what art should win the
 immortal prize,
Whose want must make life cold and Heaven
 a hollow dream?"

I looked and saw your love in the shadow of
 your heart,
As a diver sees the pearl in the shadow of
 the sea;
And I murmured, not above my breath, but
 all apart, –
"Ah! you can love, true girl, and is your
 love for me?"

As memories of so long ago flooded in, tears began to prick at the back of my eyes. It was like a forgotten dull ache suddenly being uncovered.

We discovered later, as each of us related our experiences, that none of us had wanted to come back so soon. There was so much more we wanted to know.

After talking a while Morton said, "We'll go back through the archway and you can talk again with the people you met. This time, ask them to introduce you to someone and also see if you can find out where they live."

Jimmy was waiting for me inside the archway and we walked along a country road together. I asked him to introduce me to someone and without warning there was a dog jumping and running all round us. It was a most beautiful Red Setter, so full of life, its coat a deep auburn colour and very shiny. I knew its name too. It was 'Shambles'.

I remembered then that when I knew Jimmy on this side, he was always talking about his dog, Shambles, and of how beautiful he was.

I remembered what Morton had told us to do, and said to Jimmy: *"Can you show me where you live?"*

"I don't live anywhere," he said.

Then we seemed to be travelling through the air and he showed me a narrow street with lighted taverns on either side. "*I spend a lot of time here,*" he said. And I knew it was where artists congregated to talk and drink.

Then we were climbing a tree and looking over the countryside. But at this point I heard Morton say, "It's time to say goodbye and come back to the room," and I found myself back at the

Five Kisses for a Penny

Belmont. I wanted to say goodbye to my father but could not find him. There was just a space where he had been, and beyond that – blackness. But as I looked into the blackness there appeared a pair of tired-looking, dark-green eyes. They were not the eyes of my father yet they stayed, fading only gradually, as I returned to the room.

I know now that they were the eyes of Jimmy.

A couple of weeks later at the Belmont, Morton decided we should go to the meadow as usual and meet the person we had met the previous week – in my case this was my mother.

When I reached the meadow it was to find the grass thick and luxuriant, where normally it is a lighter green and quite short. There was no one under my special tree as I walked towards it, expecting to see Mother.

This was disappointing, making me think nothing was going to happen – which is sometimes the case. We have no control over what happens on the other side, we can only think of the person we want to see and hope to make contact.

However, I continued to walk towards the tree and gradually realized someone was building up there.

It was Jimmy.

He was wearing khaki trousers and a khaki shirt with the sleeves rolled up, and he looked slimmer and taller than I remembered. He also looked serious, which I thought strange for when I had seen him the previous time he was smiling and quite different.

Morton was telling us to ask questions of the person we had met, such as: what is life like over there? What do you do? Where do you live? et cetera.

I tried asking questions but received no replies to them. The situation seemed quite unreal – perhaps because it was so unexpected.

Eventually I said: *"What do you do with yourself over here?"*

The answer came back: *"I paint. I'm painting a portrait of you."*

He showed me a white canvas standing on an easel, and painted on the canvas, in swirls of thick white paint, was a picture of billowy clouds with further clouds behind, tinged with pink, as though reflecting early morning sun.

I said, *"This is not a portrait of me!"* and he said, quite simply, *"This is how I see you."*

Morton was asking us to take our visitor by the hand and go for a walk along the river, to the waterfall.

I took Jimmy's hand and we walked towards the river and as we reached it, he put his arm round my shoulder. We walked for a little way, neither of us speaking. Then, quite suddenly, we were no longer walking by the river but walking through a churchyard in the dark.

My hands were cold and Jimmy took one and held it tight, putting it, with his, into the pocket of the greatcoat he was now wearing. I realized then, that this was a replica of something we had done in the past. We had walked home through a churchyard one night, after leaving a dance-hall.

Five Kisses for a Penny 37

On this particular night he was angry because I had danced with someone else, and although he carried my sandals home, he wasn't speaking to me.

I didn't tell him my hands were cold, and walked beside him in silence, but going through the churchyard he gripped my hand so hard that it hurt as he put our hands into his pocket.

This was what he was doing now, and my hand really hurt as we relived the scene. Then we were back walking beside the river.

We reached the waterfall, and this week it was just as beautiful as I had seen it before, but totally different. It was much higher, and masses of tumbling white water poured over the top, disappearing lower down into a fast-running stream.

"Turn round and go back to the meadow now," Morton said, "and take your visitor into your own special tree with you."

Jimmy and I arrived at my tree, but there was not enough room for us both to enter. We tried, but Jimmy had to step behind me. Then the strangest thing happened. It was as though my body was melting into his, and I could see the back-view of him at the same time as knowing his body was enveloping mine.

I raised my arms up to the branches of the tree and his arms stretched up higher than mine and my hands were hurting because he was holding them so tightly and forcing them higher than I could reach.

"Say goodbye now," said Morton.

At his words I found myself standing in the meadow – alone. Jimmy had gone and I was not able to say goodbye. It left me feeling extremely upset, knowing there was a reason for what had happened – a reason I was unable to comprehend.

Four

The situation was now changing. I was beginning to wish I could live two lives simultaneously for there was not enough time for all that I wanted to do and to think about. What was the message I was being given by Jimmy? Clearly something was wrong. Had he really died back in 1953 when he held out his hand to me at the railway station, or was he alive somewhere, in crisis, and calling me to him? It was impossible to tell.

Words like: NEVER BE DIVIDED FROM THE TRUTH BY WHAT YOU WOULD LIKE TO BELIEVE, kept coming into my mind. But what did I want to believe? I was not sure. But then on deeper examination, what I really wanted was to believe he was dead, for then 'seeing him' as I had, would make sense. If he were still alive it could mean I was fooling myself, or being fooled by my subconscious. I tried to dismiss these thoughts but there were nagging doubts at the back of my mind: I had entered the minefield of searching for knowledge and by so doing would have to negotiate the mines planted by no matter how well-intentioned fellow seekers – including those laid by my own subconscious. Was 'seeing him' just one of these mines? And if so, what did I do about it? Everywhere I went I was haunted by his eyes and the seriousness of his face until finally there was no getting away from the message: "I NEED YOU."

It was then the dreams started:

I was in a restaurant crowded with people when suddenly Jimmy and I saw each other from across the room. He pushed through the crowd and came over to where I was standing and put his arms around me. I was married but it didn't matter. All that mattered was that I was seeing Jimmy again after so many years.

We lay down on the floor of the restaurant together, not talking, just sensing; holding each other, not wanting to let go, common sense fighting a losing battle.

Soon everyone was preparing to leave. Still no words came. I knew we were in Canterbury and he was on a visit, and without thinking the question heard myself ask, "How long will you be able to stay?" and heard him answer: "46 days."

Outside the restaurant Phil stepped between us and the three of us walked down the road together, Jimmy holding my hand. Phil was angry and Jimmy upset and I knew this situation would end in disaster – I could feel a tornado of tension building.

Then Jimmy and I were out in the country and across the fields we could see people with wreaths and bunches of flowers. We thought they must be attending a funeral or maybe someone had been killed.

We began to get under strands of barbed wire set several feet apart, to see who was dead, then Jimmy said, "I'm not going to do this; I don't want to know who it is," and turned and ran away, back under the wire, down the lane, and across the fields. I knew I could never catch up with him and that I would never see him again. I knew also that his reason for running away was because he was afraid of discovering the dead person was himself.

Then I was running down a long tunnel, trying to find my way out, but where the entrance had been was a mosaic tiled door, or something completely blocking my path. There was no way of getting through so the only thing to do was go back.

The tunnel sloped downwards and the further I went the smaller it became until I was lying on my back, trying to punch a way through what was closing in on me. But as I frantically punched, pieces of wood and lumps of plaster came down on my head and I knew I was going to be buried alive: and woke up.

The next dream was different:

I was high on a mountain top, lying on the earth. All around me were bodies, dying or dead. Around us all, and right to the edge of the mountain there were soldiers with long thin swords. These soldiers were watching for the slightest movement, ready to kill whoever moved.

I was paralysed with fear for there was no escape. We seemed to be on a ledge and I knew that beyond the soldiers was a sheer drop to the sea.

After a while I was in Phil's arms. Somehow he had managed to crawl over to me and was trying to comfort and protect me. Then without any warning his body went limp and fell heavily across mine. It took some time to free myself from under his weight, and when I did, it was to discover he had been shot through the head.

I knew then that I was completely alone in this terrible situation and the shock woke me up.

Another dream ran like this:

Phil and I were asleep in bed together, Phil's body curled close around mine. Still in the dream there seemed to be someone lying between us, possibly a child, although there was no space for this. An arm from this 'child' came round my waist and I stroked the arm and turned round to embrace the child, but the arm disappeared under my fingers and I knew that the person it belonged to was dead – a person I loved and had lost.

Soon after this, as I returned to my previous position, an adult arm, Jimmy's arm, came from between us and across me. I turned again, and began stroking his naked arm, loving him and trying to ensure that he would stay. But the arm slipped away, just as the other had done and I was so distressed that I woke up.

Before the dream ended I was crying bitterly and Phil was very annoyed. The clock kept

Five Kisses for a Penny 43

blasting out music even though it was turned off. It was as though I were going mad and could not put things right no matter how hard I tried.

The middle of the night is a different country and a shattering one in which to be alone so I did the only thing I could do: I shook Phil awake. I'd run away as far as I could run and it was no longer possible to cope alone. While he cradled and comforted me, giving me courage, the panic that had been building up, and the fear of how he would react, gradually subsided. I was able to tell him what had been happening – the contacts with Jimmy – the nightmares.

I should have known better than to think he would be angry. He gently kissed my lips, hot and swollen by now, and said quietly, "There's only one thing to do. We'll start looking for him in the morning."

The logical place to begin was the Births, Marriages and Deaths department of Manchester County Council (Manchester being where Jimmy had come from when I met him in 1944 and where I assumed he would return in March 1946). From them, Phil learned that a man by the name of James Law died there in 1951, but the name we were looking for was either James Victor, or Victor James, I could not remember which, and since further information was not permitted over the telephone the girl suggested that it might be an idea to try looking for my friend through *The Manchester Evening News*. She said the paper ran an *In Touch* column; and gave us a name and telephone number.

I rang the newspaper for more detail and was told there was no charge for the *In Touch* service, but it could not be guaranteed that my search would be printed since there were so many people looking for one another.

I wrote to the editor, giving all the details I could remember, and sent him a copy of my book *A Necklace of Orange Seeds* as an incentive for including me in his column. I knew is was a very long shot and probably the only chance I would ever get of finding Jimmy: but the matter had become urgent.

About a month later, to my complete surprise, two letters arrived. One from Doreen, Jimmy's wife, telling me that he was now seventy-four years old, very weak and in a nursing home in Hereford, the other from *The Manchester Evening News* with a copy of the page on which my search story appeared. The piece was headed, "Echo of Wartime Friendship". (The name 'Echo' and the circumstances must have stirred the editor's imagination. The piece was sensitive, and beautifully presented.)

The letter from Doreen was one of welcome and I telephoned the same day to thank her for writing. She suggested that I renew my friendship with 'James', saying she was sure he would be pleased to hear from me. We had a long and pleasant conversation during which she told me she had not seen the paper herself, a relative of hers who lived in Manchester had seen it and sent her the clipping.

Although this happened only a few months ago, so much has since happened that it's difficult to remember how I felt on learning that Jimmy was still alive. There was a lot of confusion, a liberal lacing of delight and fear, and a huge spoon of trepidation for stirring the mixture. That much I can remember – and the numbness. My subconscious mind had planted a bomb – and I had been stupid enough to blow myself up.

But it was only a matter of time before I was proved wrong. Something more like a miracle had happened.

I learned from the nursing home that a few weeks prior to his being admitted, Jimmy was perfectly all right, living in a flat of his own and driving a car. It seems that he had sold his previous car for a larger model and promptly driven it into a wall. I am sure these facts are pretty condensed, but the fact that he went into a coma explained everything I needed to know. I had *not* walked into a bomb of my own planting. Jimmy's mind had contacted mine in his moments of crisis. And although I did not know why at the time, his need was so great and the urgency so strong that apart from 'seeing' him I was besieged by nightmares until finally I did what was needed: I FOUND HIM. But most astonishing of all, as I was to realize later, was the perfection with which these events had been planned and how step by step they were carried out enabling Jimmy to repay his karmic debt of past lifetimes with me.

And Phil had played no small part in all this, which was even more amazing once I learned the full extent of the roles the two men had played in these previous lives, and realized, with gradual awakening, that what I was witnessing was karmic law in effect.

On the evening of Friday, 8th April 1993, I began writing a letter to Jimmy. It was like walking in a dream. I had no idea which path to follow, how to put words together, what to say to someone who had physically passed out of my life so long ago. Neither did I have a clear idea of his condition: Would he be able to read my writing? Would whatever I wrote be read to him by somebody else? And above all: was he confused most of the time?

Phil advised me to write as though he were the same as when I last knew him, to send any photos I might have kept and to send what recent photos I had of myself.

This made sense, although when Phil and I married in 1946 I kept nothing that Jimmy and I had shared together: the sketches he did of me, the portrait in oils, the love letters, the poems, the language he was teaching me, the photographs. However, on looking through photograph albums that had passed to me on the death of my parents I discovered duplicates of some of the photos and would be able to write that I would have them copied, and send the originals. This at least was somewhere to start – something positive.

Five Kisses for a Penny 47

Unfortunately it was not possible to get anything done immediately because of the Easter Holiday and during that time another letter arrived from Jimmy's wife saying she had shown him the clipping '*Echo of Wartime Friendship*' and he had read it three times before being able to believe it. She said also that he wanted to see me as soon as possible, but didn't want me to see him the way he looked now. He wanted to try and get back on his feet a bit first, so that he could look his best. It would be a good idea she thought, knowing we were both writers, if Phil and I went up at the end of May or early in June for the Literature Festival at Hay-on-Wye, combining this with a visit to James.

Now I had enough to write about: I could say I'd be sending photographs after Easter and would be coming to see him in the summertime.

Then the dreams started again. It was as though something inside me had come unhinged and was thrashing about, for this time the dreams were accompanied by migraines: I was walking down a flight of steps and Jimmy was walking up. He stopped when we met and kissed my lips. His mouth was wet and felt disgusting. I hated it and pushed him away.

In the next dream he had come on a visit and after a while kept saying he must leave, but although he started to leave, he kept coming back. I was trying to find my camera so that I could take a picture of us together, but was unable to find it.

Then I was by myself and carrying a clear

plastic 'grip' which was filled with rice.

After each of these dreams I awoke with the familiar, flashing, zig-zagging lights of a migraine. (I have suffered migraines since early childhood but over the years they have become less severe. Now they were back in full force.)

Margaret said of the first dream, that meeting half-way on the steps meant that neither of us were getting anywhere. The kiss was 'wet and felt disgusting' because I had blanked Jimmy out of my mind after the events of years ago and persuaded myself that he didn't love me, and now that I find he does, there is a lot of confusion.

The second dream, about the camera, she said was because we are able to capture events with a camera which will stay the same years later, although we will have changed. Again, talking about the stairs, we are on different lives now and there is no way to recapture the past. I couldn't find my camera because I know there is no way of going back, even if I wanted to. But subconsciously I am back in the forties, wondering what I will think of Jimmy when I see him again – and what he will think of me. Everything on the spirit side is done in a psychological way. It's a complete psychological thought pattern. We go right to the truth in dreams and are given the answers although they may not always be what we want. And something that escapes us is always a nightmare.

The bag of rice I was carrying meant a celebration of some kind – either in this world or over the other side. "You're carrying his fate in that bag of rice," she said. "His fate is in your hands. The celebration will be according to your actions, in as much as whatever happens. He needs help and you are the only one who can help him."

I knew she was right. There had to be a reason for his contacting me and nothing so strong could be written off lightly, of this I was absolutely certain.

The migraines kept coming but the dreaming stopped. I had made up my mind what I was going to do. We would visit Jimmy in the summertime: yet somehow it didn't seem real. It was like living in the dark and seeing a vague light somewhere way out in space. Although I knew for certain that Jimmy was alive there was part of my brain which refused to believe it and stayed locked in a pool of inky-black longing. I had wandered into a world of invisible walls, without knowing how, and now I could find no way out. Of course life went on – it had to – but I wasn't with it. I was a robot performing to order, the *real* me was turned upside down, my head on the ground my heels in the air. Surely this wouldn't go on for much longer...

It didn't. On Monday, the 19th of April 1993, there came a letter from Jimmy, which miraculously set me the right way up and put everything back in perspective. Although (out of necessity) only dictated, it said everything I needed to cement the fact that he existed: "It was unexpected and marvellous to receive your letter after so many years... I will try to pen my own letter as soon as I can... you sound exactly as I remember you... I want to see you as soon as possible."

The letter was sent with all his love and somehow he had managed to sign 'Jimmy' (no matter how shakily) and followed his name with five kisses...

Five kisses for a penny – he had not forgotten how we signed all our letters, any more than I would ever forget.

Five

If things had not happened the way they did I would never be able to write this story the way it is written. For not only is it a story of love, it is a spiritual story, a story of how the spirit world can, and does help us if only we take notice. But to take notice one needs to have a little knowledge of this invisible world, to at least realize it is there, which is something so many of us never think about in the normal course of events. And yet, we are surrounded by this other world and the people in it who know what we are thinking, how we are feeling: and those on a higher level knowing what we planned for our advancement in this incarnation. And knowing also, how difficult it is for us to carry out these plans without the blueprint of previous knowledge.

Right now I am experiencing a strange yet familiar feeling. Jimmy is with me. I knew he was here when the phrase 'blueprint of previous knowledge' entered my mind for it is not what I intended to say. He is now continuing, speaking to me directly:

"Just as you are explaining, what you are writing is not only a story of love – it is a spiritual story, and this is why it is so important for me to sit and talk with you from the spirit side to ensure that you write it correctly, leaving nothing out. You can be certain I will not allow that. You will know when things are not right and you will change them. This book will leave its mark. It will go out to the public. There will be no problems.

"What I am trying to get across to you is that I needed to keep your love and had I possessed you in my life on the earthplane this time I would have lost it. I am only now understanding this myself, getting it together you might say, understanding that this is what I was subconsciously aiming at all the way through. I had to suffer this time. I had to sacrifice my happiness with the one I most endeared (you) because I owed it to you and Phil to have this lifetime together. It is what we planned in the *bardo*. The time limit given to you by Phil for choosing between he and myself was also planned, as he will discover on his return. The unknown entity was you. Only *you*, by making the right decision, could break the deadlock and allow me to repay my karmic debt. And although it was agreed at the time I now realize the difficulty of that task. I realize also, for I had forgotten, that karma does not necessarily involve punishment, it presents one with the

Five Kisses for a Penny 53

opportunity for development. We all have free will and are able to decide when and how to enlarge our understanding, our education, by doing what should be done. I chose to punish myself in this life for my transgressions in another because my need to put things right with you was so great. The act in one sense was one of selfishness, for in doing so my soul can now progress but it was not entirely selfish as I am sure you will understand.

"You may consider I broke our agreement at the end by calling out to you, but words that had to be spoken had been left unsaid and in my weakness I could not leave without receiving your forgiveness.

"You always believed your love for me was greater than mine for you. It is fortunate for me that you did. But you were oh so very wrong, and this I needed to prove to you.

"I want you now to make it clear to others that none of them are here by accident. They are here by design. And so often that design is lost through ignorance of spiritual matters and in day-to-day living, and never has the chance to be realized. Only by the experience of others who write stories such as this one can the importance of spiritual education be put before those in the greatest need of it. That is why this book will be published."

The winter afternoon light is fading and I feel caught between two worlds, a strange, strange feeling of being more than one personality yet at the same time being the sum total of a whole.

There is so much still to be learned – so much we do not yet understand. Cayce tells us that in his view we are, in some sense, living all our 'lives' at the present. A past existence is not left behind like a closed book. Full personalities develop in past lives as substructures of the present psyche. I'm sure he is right, yet perfect understanding of this is impossible without personal experience to cement the fact. Even so, facing facts is hard to come to terms with at times. Facts can so often seem like fiction if we, in our efforts to accept them, pick them apart.

On Tuesday, the 20th of April, another letter arrived from Jimmy, again dictated but to a senior member of staff at the nursing home. This letter was much longer and gave more detail of his condition. He was indeed a sick man and although he had hopes of travelling to Broadstairs to be with me it was easy to see that for him to travel any distance at all would be impossible. Because of the content of his letter, and having been told that if I telephoned the office I could be connected to his room, I decided, after much heart searching, that perhaps I could manage to hear his voice without falling to pieces. Even so, it took me a few days to 'carry my tiger to the mountain'. A strange phrase, perhaps, but one from T'ai Chi that fits perfectly, for 'carrying your tiger to the mountain – finding your point of balance' is one of the hardest things to do.

Eventually, on Tuesday 27th April, a week after Jimmy's second letter I 'carried my tiger' and lifted the telephone.

To say I was ill-prepared for what happened is a gross understatement. At first Jimmy didn't understand who I was. Then when he did, the shock of hearing my voice brought on an asthma attack so severe that a nurse who was with him had to ask if I would mind ringing back in half an hour. I knew asthma was one of his problems yet the information had not registered and was being brought home to me with a vengeance. I felt guilty, yet let down at the same time. It was not the joyous reunion I had hoped for and half and hour seemed an awful long time to wait before being able to put things right. Time, I have discovered, as doubtless many others have done, is dependent entirely upon any given situation. It can seem to pass in a flash, hang suspended or drag itself past so slowly it seems barely to be moving. In my situation it seemed to divorce me completely from reality. What was I waiting for? Had I contacted Jimmy or not? Was I going to wake up and find the dreams were starting all over again?

Then miraculously the telephone rang and I heard him say, "Echo... Echo... is that really you?"

Tears streamed down my face, I was unable to stop them. All the pent up emotion inside me melted away and had to go somewhere. Jimmy sounded *exactly* the same as he had sounded the very last time I spoke with him on that fateful day of his leaving for France – 4th January, 1946.

I don't know what I managed to reply. I can't

remember the conversation, except that he told me he was arranging to have a telephone installed in his room so that he could call me, and I him, whenever we needed to talk to each other. I remember one half of my brain telling me 'this is a seventy-four year old man on the end of the line, he's sick, and he has asthma,' and the other half refusing to believe it for his voice matched the picture of him I had in my mind – a tall handsome soldier on an April evening. Every inflection of his voice sounded the same as I remembered: the accent, the warmth, the small chuckle. How could it be possible that he was now an old man?

The whole thing is of course that we are still the same inside no matter how old we become and how ever much our outward appearance may change, the soul does not change. If we were all soul and no body we would still recognize each other, which is what happens when we pass to the other side. It is only here that we need bodies for recognition. So it is understandable that when the body is dispensed with, out of sight, like over a telephone line, all we are left with is the voice through which the soul communicates, identifying us as who we are – ourselves – without any trimmings. We never feel older or different inside. We are not as people see the outside of us. It is not until we leave this plane that we see one another as we *really* are.

I know I am not explaining this well but what I'm trying to convey is that it was a weird feeling, knowing the earthly body of a person yet hearing the voice of the soul.

The following evening, 28th April, Jimmy rang me. I had no up-to-date photographs, but hearing his voice and understanding that no matter what his appearance he was still the same person, made everything perfect. I sent him a copy of my book about Africa and every two or three days I wrote letters or sent cards to him. I reminded him of our happiness in each other: orchards and pink apple blossom; fields full of poppies, woods full of bluebells; nights filled with stars; the rain, the wind, everything I could remember us enjoying during the short times we spent together. Yet he would often surprise me when telephoning, by remembering something I had completely forgotten.

The nursing staff tried to dissuade him from having a telephone installed in his room since he was due to be moved very shortly to another home, one which could supply the extra care essential for his well-being. But they were up against a brick wall – his iron will. He would not back down and the telephone went in in a matter of days.

By now it was the beginning of May and life for me was quite hectic. I was trying to write a screen play of one of my books, which my agent in London had asked for, Phil was not well which was very worrying, Jimmy had taken a turn for the worse and daily telephone calls to and fro seemed to bring him little relief. And through it all I was getting the message that this could not go on for much longer, a climax was beginning and there was no way to stop it, all I could do was slow it down: and the best way to do this was to slow down myself.

In an effort to do this I stopped writing the play and spent time in the garden, which I knew would sew up the ragged edge of my nerves. Then with Margaret and friends from our Circle, a day spent at Stansted Hall proved to be a good tonic. Hot sunshine, a picnic and lectures from various mediums all helped to work wonders and I was ready to go back to the meditation I had so badly neglected and so sorely needed.

Life would never be the same again, I knew this to be so, but I had arrived at a point where I felt able to cope with it.

Six

At this time our Circle was meeting once a month with Margaret's guide, Chang Li, giving us direction in spiritual matters. Since the subject of past lives was in our minds we were advised to consult the Akashic Records and that someone, whose name was Daniel, would be there to help us. What follows is how I set about doing this and what I recorded as a result:

"Trying to do as Chang Li directed is proving to be extremely difficult. The Akashic Records, we have been told, are books in which every aspect of each persons' past lives is stored. I assume these books to be metaphoric, since they can hardly be otherwise, so Chang Li's suggestion that we each study ten of these books – our nearest past ten lives – needs to be done metaphorically.

"From what I have already read it would appear that there is a Universal Memory Bank, where stored information is available to those on the spirit side, and possibly to those on the earthplane who are sufficiently developed to tap into it. And this Universal Memory Bank is the record of every aspect of every persons' Total Life – Total Life meaning every incarnation from the beginning of time. So it follows that the Akashic Records and the Universal Memory Bank are one and the same thing. Nobody is writing down our every thought and act. Information is being amassed automatically, scientifically if you like: a normal, natural part of cosmic law, the way our universe operates; a great many aspects of which are still unknown to man.

"On several occasions since the Circle last week I have tried to enter the corridor where Chang Li said Daniel will be waiting to assist each of us; but have failed to get very far. The furthest I have been able to get is to see what looked more like a hazy oval tunnel than a corridor, where someone wearing a long robe stood waiting. However, when Margaret came this afternoon, we meditated together, and what transpired would indicate that more positive results are gained than when meditating alone.

"I was in a misty corridor and standing at the end of it was a figure wearing a long dark robe. When I reached the figure, I could see there was another corridor to my left and although this figure, presumably Daniel, was beside me, I could not see him.

"The Records' Room was like a huge dark vault. The ceiling was high and the walls made of stone. The whole place was filled with long rows of shelves containing large dark-covered books.

Five Kisses for a Penny 61

To the left of the shelves was a long iron ladder reaching from floor to ceiling which could be pushed along, making access to the books possible.

"As I stood looking at the top row of books which is where I assumed my ten books to be, the ladder was moved along to the end of the row, so that the tenth book would be the first to be taken. Then, although I didn't take the book down, or see it taken down, I was sitting with it across my knees; moving blocks of the pages back and forth; knowing that I was never going to be able to read all that was in it. At one stage I tried turning the pages over one by one, and although they were covered with print I could not read any of the words. I looked for pictures – but there were none.

"After a while I realized that I was out in the open, holding the bridle of a horse on which sat Jimmy. He was dressed in clothes from some other era and looked very stately. I was wearing a long dress and had a shawl round my shoulders. They were the clothes of a peasant. It was as though Jimmy was a rich man who would not deign to look at a peasant girl and my job was to stable the horses for people wanting to stay overnight at the inn. There appeared to be a number of inns – taverns – quite close together. Then without actually stabling the horse, I was up in a hay-loft above the stables, and knew that this was where I slept, and although the man on the horse had ignored me, I was nevertheless to be at his service. I knew also, that my name was Lilian.

"Strangely, although perhaps it is not so strange, my description of the Records' Room, including the ladder, tallied exactly with what Margaret had seen, including the appearance of Daniel."

Perhaps by going through the other nine books I would find out more about lives with Jimmy but there was no time then and it is irrelevant now. What *is* relevant however, is a later meditation done with Margaret after Jimmy's death, which sheds some light on the reason why it was so important for him to return this time and finally put an end to our traumatic relationships.

I mentioned in Chapter Three a past life regression with Keith Surtees in which I entered an empty room and felt unable to investigate it – there was something there I did not want to see. But it soon became evident that whatever it was could not be avoided. Parts of the jigsaw were missing and one of then lay in this room. What follows is an account of what was experienced during the finding of one particular piece:

It was a Tuesday afternoon, the curtains in my 'hut' at the top of the house were closed against the bright sunlight, which nevertheless filtered through to cover the floor with a golden glow that would not be denied behind our closed eyelids. But we concentrated together and Margaret went through the door into the empty room in my mind.

All she could see was an ornate ceiling rose, cream-coloured, surrounded by cherubs, and a

Five Kisses for a Penny

light bulb hanging from a very long cord in the centre. The ceiling resembling a parquet floor.

While she was describing this I was standing outside the door in my mind, not wanting to go through yet seeing shadowy figures behind the walls, and sensing their panic. Two women, possibly more, were scurrying about inside the room, not knowing what to do. One was small and old and wearing an apron.

Because of not wanting to be involved and because of my fear I took myself away from the situation and floated my mind on a smooth blue lake surrounded by mountains – it's a place I've invented and find very peaceful for meditation.

Then, without knowing how, I was actually right *in* the room and it was obvious why there was trouble. Lying on a big four-poster bed, was a girl. She was fully dressed and had long blonde hair. It was as though she had flung herself back in desperation, one arm hanging from the side of the bed. I knew she was dead and that the blame would be placed on these women who would be held responsible for her death. This was why I could feel their panic.

The girl on the bed was me, devoid of emotion, except for a feeling of peace that was gradually growing.

I did not want to stay and witness this scene and somehow managed to get back to my lake. Then quite suddenly something swept me back to the room and I could see a man standing, big and strong, in the doorway. He was very, very angry. I knew this man was Jimmy although I could not see his face. The women were trying to explain what had happened, but he would not listen and ordered them out.

I decided to leave too but was drawn back by an overwhelming knowledge of sadness. There, inside the room, the man was now kneeling beside the bed, holding the dead girl's hand and sobbing. He was utterly heartbroken. It came to me then that I had ended my life by taking poison. Not because I didn't love him but because of the situation that had been forced upon me – a situation with which I was unable to cope. I wondered what year this had taken place and was given '1869'.

Margaret said it seemed to her that one of us had left a fortune because of love – had left a lot of stability. She had gained the same impression as me, that the girl had women to look after her and yet the conditions were impoverished. The lone bulb on a long cord was symbolic of the girl ending her life. She was obviously very much alone. There was no way out except death.

I'm sure there must be more to this story but there is no point in pursuing it. It does show however, that I am not entirely blameless in my encounters with Jimmy through various lifetimes for although he has hurt me a number of times, I have also, for whatever reasons, hurt him.

It is not a comfortable feeling to learn you have hurt someone and I found it difficult to forget what I'd seen. Logic was telling me it was stupid to dwell on the past for nothing could change what had already happened, there were no roads back. There was only one road, and that went forward.

I wrote more letters and sent more cards but telephone calls from Jimmy became fewer, and those that I made to him were not successful: he was usually in the day-room from where he was brought to his room in an agitated condition, his being moved having taken a lot of his strength. It had the effect of making me dubious of lifting the phone for fear of causing him problems yet at the same time knowing that if I did not, he would think I no longer cared.

The beginning of the end came on Tuesday, 11th May, when a letter arrived from Jimmy's wife giving me details of a different nursing home to which he had been moved. He was in Room 6 of the Garden Wing which would give him a brighter outlook and where he would receive the extra care he now needed. There was a new telephone number for contacting him.

Although this news was ominous it didn't really sink in for I could not believe that anything drastic would happen. I had promised to see him and knew he believed me; therefore he would wait for the summer when he knew I was coming. There was even a chance that with new surroundings and extra treatment his physical state would improve, and there was certainly nothing wrong with his mind. I continued to send letters and cards as usual and began again to make telephone calls, and he did indeed seem very much better.

During the next few weeks there were many commitments which occupied much of my time yet concentration was difficult. Always, hovering above me, was a cloud of indefinable density. Sooner or later I would have to face facts: Jimmy was approaching the end of his stay here and before this happened it was imperative that I reach him.

Life became a juggling act – a race against time.

Seven

All through the next month I had the strangest feeling that I'd been swept into a looking-glass world where time and emotions were visible colour and telephone calls their only connection. When days went by without a connection I would people the void with phantoms. Suppose this looking-glass world were the real world, and all that had happened was only a dream, what would I do then? What would I do if the telephone calls were imagined and there was no real live person on the end of the line? Could I walk away from this dream as though nothing had changed and still remain the same person? What happens to thoughts and plans that are left in mid air?

There was no answer to these questions and fortunately no answer was needed. The days had marched on to the 19th of June and a Psychic Fair on that day was our final commitment. Suddenly my life resumed its normal perspective. We were free to travel to Hereford. I could now make a positive statement. We would leave Broadstairs on the 22nd and be with Jimmy on the 23rd. Even so, I was almost afraid to tell him in case something went wrong. On Sunday, the 20th, everything around me seemed to collapse. It was as though all the time I was forced to keep going I had been able to cope and now that the pressure was off there was nothing to hold me together. I was filled with the fear that I would not reach him in time, that something dreadful was about to happen; I must forget about plans for the future for what future there was could be counted in days.

Sometime previously there had been a letter telling me that his condition was such that he had only a short time to live, and although the news was extremely upsetting I had been unable to believe this was so. How could he think the way he was thinking and say the things that he said if he was dying? I suppose I though I had magical powers, that by doing everything I could possibly do, and giving all I could possibly give he would, by some miracle, regain health and strength and return to his normal self – even to driving his car. Now I was sure this would never happen.

That evening before telephoning Jimmy I spoke to the Sister on duty who confirmed my worst fears: he was a very sick man living only for my letters and phone calls, it was a wonder he hadn't gone long ago but his spirit was strong and he wouldn't give in.

"I'll be with you in a few days time," I told him when he finally answered my call to his room. "I'll

Five Kisses for a Penny

be there on the morning of Wednesday, the 23rd of June."

For a few agonized seconds, or a hundred years, all I could hear was his laboured breathing until he said in a strained, strangled voice, "I'll wait for you then. I'll hang on till you come."

I wound back the sound of previous conversations, noting the tone of his voice in detail, the tone of mine; noting my frame of mind and judging the frame of his. The world had changed shape and we had changed with it and now we were puppets performing to order. The last act of the play had already begun and the hands of fate were in charge of the strings.

June this year was an exceptionally wet month, yet the morning of the 22nd dawned bright and clear as Phil and I left home. And as the day progressed the sun, that had forgotten to shine for so long, drenched us with hours of comforting warmth. The world looked so beautiful and fresh and new that it was difficult to accept our reason for travelling. I knew what to expect when we arrived in Hereford, but it didn't make sense. Nobody could be sick and dying on a day such as this. I had made a mistake – that was the answer. But six and a half hours later when we checked in at the Hopbine Hotel, which was not much more than a stone's throw from Jimmy, I was back down to earth. My phone call to him was catastrophic. He was unable to hear or understand what I said and eventually I was forced to end the call, then ring again and speak to the Sister who could go to his room and explain that I would see him at 10 o'clock the next morning.

With nerves stretched to breaking point Phil and I somehow got through the night, neither of us knowing what to expect. Phil wanted to protect me from whatever shock was in store. I didn't know what I wanted except that I wished today were tomorrow for the waiting would then have been over, and the worst have been faced.

We went down to breakfast but coffee was all we could manage and at 9 o'clock Phil went by himself to the nursing home.

Less than half an hour later he was back at the hotel, a radiant look on his face. "I've seen him," he said, holding me tight, "he looks much better than I expected and he gave me a beautiful smile." Then he looked puzzled. "But there's something strange going on," he continued. "I know that I know him, yet I've never seen him before. And he knows me too because he said: 'Good to see you again Phil, good to see you'."

Over the next forty-eight hours strange things were to happen yet it was only afterwards their strangeness was realized for during these hours the three of us were in a different dimension where everything that was said and done appeared perfectly normal. We were experiencing an altered state of consciousness without being aware of the transition.

My meeting with Jimmy at 10 o'clock was a moment in time that is hard to forget. He was sitting so still, watching the door as I entered the day-

Five Kisses for a Penny

room. There were other people around but all I could see was him. Sun streamed through open French windows, and as I walked to his chair and he looked up at me the whole of the garden, all green and gold, seemed to be in his eyes. Time hung suspended. He took my hands and pressed them to his lips, his eyes never leaving my face. There was utter silence. No words were spoken, yet those unspoken words were filling up volumes and filling his eyes till they overflowed.

Then the world stepped back in, and carried on around us as though nothing had happened. Someone brought coffee and biscuits. Patients were wheeled into the sunshine. Music poured from a radio. Nurses chattered and laughed. It was all going on in the background as I sat in an armchair beside him and we began putting the pieces of our separate lifetimes into some sort of picture to show to each other. The world appeared to be solid and normal but we knew it was only an illusion. The *real* world was the one he was going to, and the only truth; that I would be left in this world of illusion until it was my time to join him.

Thinking of it now, perhaps strangest of all was that it seemed as though we had never been parted. There was no dense thicket separating strangers. It was as if we had walked out of one door and in through another with no time between. I put a quartz crystal into his hand and he said, "It's like the one you gave me before." But I had never given him a crystal. I asked if he liked it and he said, "Of course I do. I like everything you do for me. Nobody ever looked after me like you did." This statement didn't seem odd at the time, but it *is* odd, because I've never looked after him – at least, not in this lifetime.

We talked about Africa and *A Necklace of Orange Seeds* that I wrote as a result of what happened out there and he said, "I never thought you would write a book like that. I could talk about that time forever, but we don't need to go any further. There was an awful lot of tension in Africa but it all worked out for the best."

He was talking as though he had been there with me in the lifetime in Africa when Phil was N'doko the warrior, and I was Warengaro. Could Jimmy have been Geoffrey, my father, who fought N'doko so long and so ardently for possession of me? The more I think of it the more it makes sense. 'These two men have crossed swords in many lifetimes' I was told in the past life regression with Keith Surtees, recounted earlier in this book. But when Ivor James took me back to Africa, and figures began to build up I refused to go through that lifetime again. Apart from not wanting to experience the trauma, I must have subconsciously known who the main characters would be and therefore didn't need to have it repeated.

Again about Africa Jimmy stated, "You loved Africa, didn't you. I did too, but it had to end for there to be another beginning."

Later, and nothing to do with Africa, he was examining my bracelets, and the rings on my fingers, especially the solitaire diamond. "I see

Five Kisses for a Penny 73

you're still wearing my ring," he said. "You always loved diamonds."

This was true. I have always loved diamonds, and because I especially wanted a large solitaire I had seen when in London, Phil bought it for me, although he had already given me other diamonds. Perhaps at some time Jimmy had given me a solitaire, which would account for my passionate longing, but it was certainly not in this lifetime. Neither of us had anything this time round except a few stolen months in the middle of a war.

At lunchtime Phil came to collect me for a picnic lunch in the grounds of the Hopbine. He had been into the town and bought freshly baked bread; wine, tomatoes and cheese, a bag full of fruit. It all seems like a fairy tale now: lush green grass; hot sunshine; the food; Phil's concerned loving voice as he talked about Jimmy and me with deep understanding. I needed Phil's nearness and understanding without knowing the need, and these were the gifts that he gave, knowing me better than I know myself.

About an hour later we went back to the nursing home. Phil sat in the garden with his work – a book he was writing. I took up my seat beside Jimmy. He looked different from the way he had looked in the morning. His eyes were perfectly still, their faraway gaze suggesting that his mind was engaged with matters elsewhere, matters of which he alone was aware.

"Where did you spring from?" he said

suddenly, shifting his gaze. "I was just painting a portrait of you but it was all pink and white clouds."

How could I say that his mind had already shown me this portrait during one of the times I had seen him while meditating at the Belmont? How could I explain something to him that I could not properly explain to myself? All I could say was: "It's a portrait you're going to paint later on, that's why it's in your mind now. It's the way that you'll think of me but you don't know it this minute."

The words sounded strange as I said them and they were not the words I intended to say, but he smiled and said nothing, just held my hands tight and kissed them.

Shortly after this he slept for a while and I joined Phil in the garden. Later, when Jimmy awoke, he said he wanted to be in his room, he had a picture there that he wanted to give me. I went in search of the nurses because he was agitated. They gave him pain killers and settled him comfortably on top of his bed. "They don't understand me," he said. "They think I'm stubborn and stupid. They won't do anything I ask, besides, I wanted to give you the picture myself."

There were several pictures on the walls of his room, all of which were his own creations. One was especially lovely, a detailed painting of a bluebell wood. I told him I thought he was a wonderful artist and he laughed and said, "Piffle." I laughed with him as I examined the others because he was entirely wrong and he must have known it.

Then I was silent, shocked into silence by a sepia sketch, a three-quarter length sketch of an attractive young woman, naked from the hips up, her body beautifully curved; breasts in perfect proportion; head thrown back; hands under her hair: just the glimpse of an eyebrow to prove she was me. I looked at the bottom right of the picture and read Jimmy's signature and the date: 'James Law, 53'. I could hardly believe it.

"That is the picture I want you to have," he said, "take it down from the wall so that I can give it to you."

I did as he said and handed it to him. He looked at it for a minute and said, "I called her 'Dorothea' because I couldn't use your name or the name that I gave you. Various issues of prints were done and they sold very quickly... they were..." The unfinished sentence hung in the air as he put the framed picture into my hands.

The next moments are difficult to describe for everything went into slow motion. I thanked him without any words and put my hand on his cheek. Our eyes searched each other's. The nightmare I had had of him at the railway station, holding out his hand to me, crawled through my brain as I remembered it happened the year of this picture – 1953 – seven years after we parted. For some reason he had needed me then and had contacted me the only way possible and I had been ignorant at that time of spiritual matters and unable to respond. I have learned since that I should have taken his hand. No harm would have befallen me and he would have been comforted. But it was too late now to turn back the clock.

"May I take it home with me?" I managed to say.

"What do you mean, may you?" he said. "It's yours! I did it for you!"

The rest of the afternoon is mainly a blur. There were times he slept lightly, waking up to call out, "Don't go. Stay with me. I don't want anyone else," and I would say, "It's all right... It's all right... I'm here – I'm here."

One time he said, "I don't understand all this. Why is it happening to us? We don't deserve this – we really don't."

I soothed him as best I could. There were bouts of laboured breathing and coughing. I called a nurse. She said he would be all right. Each time he called out I said something to calm him and he responded to my voice. But when he became desperate and called out, "Why is this happening to you and me? I love you, I love you. Stay with me. Don't leave me alone," I knew it was time to do something else and free him from whatever was going on in his mind.

"Jimmy, Jimmy," I called gently, touching his shoulder. "Wake up, wake up. Let's talk, shall we?"

"Where's my crystal?" he asked, in a perfectly normal voice.

"It's in your hand. Look. You're holding it in your hand," I said, pointing to where it was.

He took my hand and began moving my

Five Kisses for a Penny 77

solitaire diamond, watching it sparkle.

"It's pretty, isn't it?" I said. "Diamonds are pretty."

"That's not what I'm trying to say and you know it," he said, his voice a rebuke. "It was *my* ring. The ring that I gave you."

I changed the subject by talking about Canterbury but it was difficult to hold his attention and every few minutes he interrupted what we were saying by asking, "What time is it?"

Each time he asked I felt cold inside for it was as though he were checking off what hours were left to him. I felt helpless and sad, for the journey that was coming would have to be made alone, and there was nothing I could do to prepare him for it: nothing that anyone could do.

In the dining room of the Hopbine that evening the table where Phil and I sat seemed suspended in space. Nothing was real. We ate our meal but our thoughts were not there. I suppose we'd dispensed with our usual functions and slipped without knowing into automation, a natural safety-valve for minds locked in overdrive.

When the night came it was not quite so bad as the previous one we'd experienced. We had accepted the day in our separate ways and there was a certain calmness in knowing the worst: except that the clock, with its loud lonely tick, was throwing me pictures of Jimmy alone in his bed, counting the hours and the minutes until he ran out of time.

Eight

Early next morning I had a short vivid dream. It began with a tree. It was only a small tree, brilliantly dressed in autumn colours but each leaf was vibrant and so joyously alive that the shape of the tree was constantly changing. There was something unusually familiar about it and I knew I had seen it in some other place, although I couldn't remember just where.

Then I was swimming way out to sea in pale shallow water which suddenly changed colour and became very deep, as it does when one swims over the edge of a reef. A moment later I was hovering above a glorious garden. It was filled completely with flowers, especially enormous white daisies with no space between them, and no room for more, yet nothing was crowded. Then I rose higher, above all of this, and was surveying the countryside as a whole. And everywhere I looked there was colour, breath-taking colour, like nothing I've ever experienced before. The shades of blue were incredibly lovely and defy

Five Kisses for a Penny

any description I could possibly give for they produced inside me a feeling of ecstasy – and how can a feeling such as this be described?

After a while I noticed a field with a hedge down one side behind which ran a lane. And as I was watching, two horses appeared side by side, gliding in perfect unison. One was jet black and the other a brilliant blue, the same even colour all over, making them look like painted horses, too smooth to be real, yet they were real enough to me in the dream and as vibrantly alive as the tree and the flowers. I moved on from there and saw below me a group of women and children playing games in a street made of pink paving-stones. I went down to join them and suddenly knew that this was the place where the tree belonged. This was where I had seen it before.

I turned round to look for the tree and there it stood, glowing in all of its glory as much as to say: Yes, this is where I belong and you *have* been here and seen me before.

This was a marvellous revelation and just what I needed for it showed me that I was not dreaming, but astral travelling in the beautiful country from which we all come, and where Jimmy would be returning before very long. This was something positive to hang on to during the uncertainty of the coming day, something with which I could comfort him should it be necessary. He was not a man to engender pity. With a spirit so strong, to offer him pity would be an insult. But for even the strongest among us, being rendered helpless is difficult to bear, and I would need all the help I could get if I were to keep up his courage.

Although Jimmy's situation was grave I did not feel depressed. I felt thankful. Thankful that we were together again, that we had been given this chance to put everything right, to say the things we had been unable to say because of the way we had parted. It was like writing the satisfactory end of a story, a bizarre yet 'happy ever after' ending in its own special way. I would go away and not see him again, we both knew that, but it didn't matter. He would be going away too, much further than I would be going just yet. We knew that also, but it was not important. The only important thing was what we had *now,* for nothing could take that away.

It may seem a strange thing to say, but at breakfast Phil and I were both happy. The morning was sweet and clean, the dining-room windows open, the sun promising the diners another hot day as they greeted each other with cheerful voices. Perhaps this had been the scene the previous morning and our emotional turmoil had rendered us blind and deaf to it. A phrase ran through my mind: 'Never throw yourself off a cliff just because you happen to find yourself at the edge of one.' Yesterday morning we had been at the edge of a cliff; but there was no cliff today.

It was too early to see Jimmy so Phil took me with him to a supermarket in town for the makings of a picnic such as we had enjoyed the previous day, then left me at the nursing home

Five Kisses for a Penny 81

and went back to the hotel to collect his work.

Jimmy was already in the day-room and watching the door as I entered. I thought he looked tired but the smile he gave me lit up his face and the expression I had seen completely vanished, or perhaps I had imagined it there in the first place. I don't know how to describe the way I was feeling. It was as if I were stranded in mid-air and not in command of my senses; as if I couldn't trust what I was seeing or feeling; as though I would be suddenly snatched away from being with him and dumped in some foreign place. The sensation was only momentary for as soon as I reached his chair and kissed his cheek my feet touched the ground: he was solid and real and so was I and we had the whole of the day to spend together.

There was a lot of noise going on in the room and Jimmy became breathless, trying to say all he wanted to say, trying to fit the years we had been apart into what few hours were left. He told me that when he returned from France after the war he had gone to Thanington looking for me. He had seen my mother and tried to fit together the 'bits and pieces' that had happened to me while he'd been away. He wanted to form a picture of the events that led to our parting but the picture he received was not what he wanted. There was no satisfactory answer for what had gone wrong.

"I wanted to find you," he said. "I couldn't let you think I had just let you go without fighting to keep you. You were mine. I wanted to take you from Phil but I didn't know where you had gone and no one would tell me."

"It's over now. Don't get upset," I told him. This is only one of our lives. We have had lives before and there are others to come. I'll be with you then."

"You've *got* to be with me," he said. "I can't be without you."

I held his hands to make him feel calmer and he smoothed each of my fingers, examining the nail varnish.

"Pink pearl," I said cheerfully, "pink pearl. Do you like it?"

He didn't answer in words. The tears in his eyes told me he was lost and alone and the feel of my hands was all he had left to hold on to.

Phil came in from the garden and the moment passed. The men smiled at each other and Jimmy said, "You cut down a lot of trees in Africa when you were clearing the forest for the iron birds of the white people."

There was silence as the three of us looked at each other. What Jimmy had just said proved beyond doubt that we had shared other lifetimes together, for this was from the lifetime I had written about in *A Necklace of Orange Seeds*. Phil had indeed cut down a lot of trees for the iron birds of the white people, when he was the warrior, N'doko.

It is one thing to believe in reincarnation but quite another to have it brought home so forcibly. I felt again as I had in the Congo, that I'd stepped into another dimension, only this time I wasn't blind to the memory. Even so, it was

Five Kisses for a Penny 83

disquieting.

Phil went back to his work in the garden and Jimmy looked as though his eyes had gone off into some other time, some other place. "I've known Phil before," he said quietly. "Do you think he can give me a new body?"

"You're going to have a new body, a lovely new body," I told him, when I'd swallowed the shock of the question. "You'll feel so good you won't know yourself. You're going to be very surprised."

"I liked your mum and dad," he said, out of context. "They were always nice to me. I'd like to see them again. Do you want to come with me?"

I didn't know how to answer him. Clearly he was preparing his leaving and would not be here for much longer. "I'd love to come with you," I managed to say, "but I've got an important book to write first. I'm going to write our story."

"I was always going to write about us," he said, "so I can put you on the right track. We'll write our story together." (Words I was to find of great significance.)

He was back with me now, not locked away in a world of his own. He was even quite cheerful. "I'm not quite sure I've got the hang of all this," he smiled, "but I believe what you've told me, and I've always got your crystal."

Most of the time after lunch Jimmy seemed to be dreaming, a slow small smile occasionally appearing on his face. Every so often he squeezed my hand and half opened his eyes, making sure I was still there, although I have understood since that what he was really doing was making sure he was still with me – that the slender thread between us was not yet broken.

It was a strange yet peaceful feeling, being the lifeline for a man hovering so near to the next world while still remaining in this; a peaceful, privileged feeling, to be sharing these moments by giving what only *I* was able to give him, knowing that I was all that he wanted.

It made me feel humble in the face of something almighty.

Late in the afternoon, as shadows began to lengthen in the garden, Phil came in to say it was time we were leaving. Jimmy half raised himself and gave him a smile: "It's been good seeing you again Phil," he said. "Good seeing you."

Phil shook his hand. "Take care of yourself old chap. Remember she loves you." He patted Jimmy's shoulder and turned to me saying, "Just take your time. I'll wait for you in the car."

"I have to leave you now," I told Jimmy slowly. "We have to go home in the morning, but I'll keep writing letters. And I'll send the book I've got on order for you – the book called *Life Between Life*. It will give you answers to all the questions you've asked me and we haven't had time to talk about."

I kissed his lips and he held my face in his hands – the repeat of a parting down a long tunnel of time, and like all those years ago, neither of us could say the word 'good-bye'.

I pulled gently away from him, our eyes still

Five Kisses for a Penny 85

holding on to each other. "I'll be waiting to meet you," he said, the unshed tears in his voice. "Don't ever forget I'll be waiting to meet you."

I knew, as I took myself away from him, that I would never see him again in this lifetime, and those words he had spoken, would be the last I would ever hear.

I didn't feel hungry at dinner. It wasn't possible to swallow the food. The distance until I would see Jimmy again could only be measured in light-years, that was all I could think of – and feel. I knew it was stupid. I could have saved myself all the heartache if I'd been content to leave things alone. He was just down the road and I could get up and run to him if I wanted to, but it wouldn't solve anything, some time or other I would have to come back and when good-byes have been said, even without any words, it's best to be strong and leave it that way.

I looked over at Phil. Like mine, the food on his plate was untouched. His eyes were heavy and dark with unspoken questions.

"There's nothing to say," I said, looking straight at him. "It's just that I know what's going to happen and I feel a bit shattered right now."

He pushed back his chair and walked round the table to move mine. "Let's walk in the garden for a while," he said. "I feel the same way as you. This experience is something I wasn't bargaining for. I can't help respecting the enemy although he isn't my enemy now."

We discussed the bewildering aspects of all that had happened, bewildering for Phil because he'd been hit by emotions that until now had lain dormant inside him. He had not expected to be drawn into a spiritual whirlpool and practically drowned.

"I'm sorry for all that has happened," I said, holding his hand. "It's been hard on you. I know that."

"You're wrong, very wrong," he told me. "This has been a great comfort to me. It's proved that I'm never going to lose you. It's proved that what happened in Africa, really *did* happen, that we *were* there before, and this life we have now will not be the last. If I have to share you with Jimmy – so what – he's one hell of a nice guy."

That evening we met Steve, Jimmy's son. I had telephoned Steve and his sister Vicky the previous evening, hoping to arrange a meeting with them for that is what Jimmy wanted. It was astounding that he had named his children *Vicky* and *Stephen,* although after all that had happened between us it should not have surprised me. It was merely more evidence of the linking of minds. For soon after Phil and I married and were expecting our baby, we decided on calling her Vicky. However, we didn't have Vicky, we had a son, and the name we chose for our son was Stephen – now a fully grown man known as Steve... My diary for 1946–47 is full of waiting for Vicky – then a son being born and our naming him Stephen.

Jimmy's son Steve, came to the Hopbine to meet us. Naturally he wanted to talk of his father but also about sailing and Africa, two subjects close to his heart – and close to ours. I was amazed at the kindness shown me by Jimmy's family. They were much more civilized than most people might have been under the circumstances, their only concern being for 'James' and his needs. Unfortunately we were not able to meet Jimmy's daughter or wife; one lived too far away and the other was in hospital. But at least we were able to express our gratitude and to talk with his son.

Steve arrived about eight o'clock. I had wondered how I would feel if he looked like the memory of Jimmy still walled-up in my mind, and how I would cope if this were the case, for I was confused enough as it was. But I need not have worried. I had forgotten he was the product of a different generation and would not necessarily look the same. Certainly there were similarities: the same easy grace, the magnetic personality; but there the similarity ended. He was a person in his own right and therefore very refreshing. He spoke lovingly of his father, of sailing, and a happy family life, so whatever Jimmy may have felt at times, he kept to himself. Steve told us of his walking through Africa and I wondered if the love that he had for this country had come genetically to him from his father. There is still so much to be learned about genetics and cosmic law and cause and effect that the mind boggles even to think about it.

Several pleasant hours later we took Steve the

short distance to his home. Then slowly drove back to the hotel and sat watching from the bedroom window, the transparent darkness of a June midnight gradually give way to the pinkness of dawn.

It was the closing chapter of our stay at Hereford.

Nine

Early on Sunday morning, the 27th of June 1993, two days after our leaving Hereford, the telephone rang in our house in Broadstairs. The sound was ominous. Nobody calls anyone so early on a Sunday with news that is good.

I picked up the phone.

"Dee?"

"Yes."

"It's Steve." The words were soft. "My father died a few hours ago... I thought you would like to know..."

For a moment I was unable to think, then heard myself saying, "Yes... Yes, thank you..."

"We had a call from the home very early and my sister and I were with him when he died. He was holding your crystal all the time. I thought he would want you to know that." The words came pouring over the line as though a flood-gate had opened, yet his voice was calm and controlled.

There was a short pause, then he said, "It was just as if he'd been hanging on till he saw you."

I felt weak inside and wondered if Steve felt the same and was putting up a brave front. It must be far worse for him than for me. I tried to be strong. "He said he would hang on... they were the exact words he used..." My voice started cracking.

"Are you all right?" His sounded concerned.

"Yes... Yes, thank you. Thank you for telling me."

"I'll write... when things settle down a bit..."

It was as though he were comforting me. I knew it should be the other way round, I should be doing the comforting, but I couldn't think of the right words to say. There was a big black hole where my brain should have been, a hole that was growing bigger.

"Jimmy's dead, isn't he." It was a statement from Phil – not a question. He took the phone out of my hand and replaced it in its holder. "We were expecting it, weren't we..." His voice was soft. I felt like a stone statue. He put his arms round me. "He's much better off where he is now, he couldn't go on as he was."

"I know... It's just such a shock..."

He cradled me close to his chest and something melted inside me. "Just let it out," he said gently. "You don't have to be brave in front of me."

Tears started to flow. Irrational? Of course it was irrational, but it was no good telling myself that.

Phil drew the curtains, locked the doors and poured me a drink. "We'll hole up together today and shut out the world," he said. "I lost him too,

Five Kisses for a Penny 91

so I know how you feel."

By this time I was sobbing. He held me tight and cried with me. I shall never forget that day, the warmth, the closeness, the love; the way we clung together and cried ourselves out. Perhaps that's the best way of dealing with grief: crying yourself out with someone who cries with you. I had always thought that in grief I would want to hole up alone, but I was entirely wrong. There is no therapy in being alone – it only prolongs the agony.

I don't remember the rest of the day or what time we went to our bed, but that night I dreamed I was riding in the back of a long black car, and looking out of the window saw an archway of most beautiful pink roses. The flowers were in full bloom and so many were clustered together that the whole mass, rising to a point above the archway, was vibrating with life and colour.

Then I was standing in the garden of a house in which Phil and I had been living and which we had decided to sell. The earth was black and freshly dug over in preparation for replanting. To the right of the garden rose a steep, grassy bank, where young trees bathed in sunshine were growing.

Looking back into the garden I was surprised to see three big old tree stumps where there had been nothing before, and from these stumps, well-established new trees were growing, tall and straight. Over the whole garden there was now what looked like a canopy and I thought how lovely and shady it was and wondered why we should be leaving such a beautiful place.

On relating this dream to Margaret she questioned me closely as to whether it was before or after I learned of Jimmy's death. Then she said: "A garden is always a peaceful thing – the roses mean love, so you're getting confirmation that James has gone to the spirit side peacefully. And you've obviously related that familiar place you knew and lived in with Phil at some time because you felt great contentment there at one point, and you've picked up this one point and been allowed to share it with him.

"James is confirming that he's fine. And the three old tree stumps with straight new trees growing from them, means that you and Phil will be joining him – in this new garden. The three of you together, because you have chosen for this to happen.

"There is going to be a lot more for you to write about through James on the spirit side, perhaps because he knew Phil when he spoke to him. It seems that it's through James that Phil will become more aware. We have already been told that he will, even though he doesn't know it yet. James will do it in his own way."

Margaret went on to say, "James has done the suffering more, he has gone through his karmic rule as far as you are concerned, because of the differences that were between him and Phil before. What's happened in the past is that he has had the opportunity of having you as his love, and everything else we know, and that he's abused it. He's put you through a lot of problems

Five Kisses for a Penny 93

in more ways than one so in this lifetime I feel that he's owed it to you to be away from you. But in his being away from you, his love has been so strong that he's suffered."

(This ties up with what I have learned over the past few months of meeting Jimmy again.)

"Now that James has gone he's managed to have his soul settled by you being there prior to his passing. He's held on because it was important for him to have gone through the lifetime without contacting you, which he did. He did *not* contact you. But he needed to know, when he knew it was his time to leave, that you still cared for him as much as he cared for you. And so he's gone over peacefully because that's happened. You have taken the love that he offered you.

"As far as Phil is concerned he carried out his duty as well. He's been your protector *from* James. The lesson learned, is that in your last lifetime with James you were obviously devastated. I don't know how you passed in that lifetime, but I would imagine it was a very sad scene, with Phil there to comfort you."

Since Margaret told me these things I have learned from Jimmy, and from past life regressions, which I have already related, that she was not far out in her speculations. I have also learned something that completely astounds me: In Chapter Four I related a dream in which Jimmy visited me in Canterbury and when asked how long he could stay, he replied, "46 days." Later in this dream we were out in the country and across the fields could see people with wreaths and bunches of flowers. We thought they must be attending a funeral and were anxious to know whose it was.

As we began to get under strands of barbed wire to cross the fields and see who was dead, Jimmy said, "I'm not going to do this. I don't want to know who it is," and turned and ran away, back under the wire, down the lane, and across the fields.

I knew in the dream that I could never catch up with him and that he was running away because he was afraid of discovering the dead person was himself.

Thinking of this now, I realize exactly what I was being told: that once the run down began (when Jimmy was moved to the new nursing home) he would have 46 days to live. And although at the time of the move he was not conscious of this, he already knew it subconsciously, because in the dream he knew the dead person was himself, just as *I* knew it. So the dream was not really a dream, it was his subconscious mind relaying a message to mine – the same sort of thing as when his mind has contacted mine at various other times in my life: most forcibly when he needed me most – when he knew that his end was approaching.

In the normal course of events we pay little attention to our subconscious minds, but there is no doubt that the subconscious is far in advance of what is normally needed for everyday living, and its language and method of communication, far finer and more complex than we in our earthbound bodies are able to comprehend – except in moments of crisis.

In going through my diary of events as they happened, I have concrete evidence that from the time I learned Jimmy had gone to the new nursing home, and the day that he died, is *exactly* 46 days.

On Monday, the 28th of June, the book *Life Between Life* that I had ordered for Jimmy, arrived. It came as a shock for the events of the previous day had anaesthetised my mind. Now long dark passageways were beginning to appear, down which my thoughts were straining to run, and the words 'He won't be needing it now', stood twenty feet high in my mind, blocking the way. Then, as I stood helplessly holding the book in my hands, and wondering what to do with it, I heard Jimmy say: "Send it to Steve he might need it one day, and also I want him to have my crystal."

I felt at that moment as though I'd been pulled to pieces and just as quickly put back together again.

A few wilderness months passed before I was ready to begin telling this story, but the rich tapestry has always been there, I just needed to have it brought to my notice: whatever heartache and pain there has been in my life there has always been love to equal the balance. Love is the driving force. Without love there is nothing. This is something we all understood in the *bardo* but had forgotten when we came back to the earthplane for the men to settle their differences and make progress.

But we were incredibly lucky, for the world of spirit stepped in and heightened our senses during the short time the three of us spent together. We were able to look into that *Life Between Life* and remember the plans we had made. What did it matter that these two men loved one woman? What was the point in fighting each other when there was no hate or jealousy where we had come from and where we'd eventually be staying? For each individual is a separate soul with freedom of choice, and no one wants to own, or belongs exclusively to, anyone else.

Because of ignorance and misunderstanding, through many incarnations we shared poignant sorrow. And now at last we share profound peace.

So there's an important message to be learned from this story: Life gives you back exactly what you put into it, and if you have not accomplished all that you came here to do, there is always another chance to start over.

And no one can ask for better than this...